THE
SYMBOLS AND LEGENDS
OF
FREEMASONRY.

BY

J. FINLAY FINLAYSON.

SECOND EDITION.

THE BOOK TREE
San Diego, California

Second Edition
Originally published 1910
by
George Kenning & Son
London

New material, revisions and cover
© 2003
The Book Tree
All rights reserved

ISBN 1-58509-241-X

Published by
The Book Tree
P O Box 16476
San Diego, CA 92176
www.thebooktree.com

We provide fascinating and educational products to help awaken the public to new ideas and information that would not be available otherwise.
Call 1 (800) 700-8733 for our *FREE BOOK TREE CATALOG*.

INTRODUCTION

Freemasonry is a secret mystical brotherhood that dates back many centuries. According to the author it teaches of the possibility that an inner principle of life is found within us and survives bodily death, and that a Great Architect of the Universe exists. It also seeks to unite its members in the great brotherhood of man.

These important teachings are conveyed through legends and symbols that are laid out clearly in this book. It covers secrets and symbols from ancient India, Chaldea, Egypt, Judea, Greece, Italy, Germany and England, plus a chapter on Modern Freemasonry. It includes 48 illustrations in 15 separate plates and covers such subjects as the all-seeing eye, immortality of the soul, the mystery of death, Biblical Masonry, Solomon's temple, the Greater Mysteries, the Essenes, Christian Masonic symbols, Freemasons of the Renaissance, Sun worship, symbolic architecture, Hiram Abif and much, much more.

This book starts from remote history and brings us up through the ages, revealing the secrets as it goes. Before this modern printing this rare book remained unavailable and out of print for almost a century. With this information available once again, we are now able to understand more fully what certain symbols really mean and where they came from. One may also be enlightened in the same way regarding various legends from around the world, Freemasonic and otherwise. Finlayson reveals interesting information on every page, which makes this book a must for Masonic members, or equally interesting to all those seeking knowledge in mythology, symbols and legends.

Paul Tice

PREFACE.

I AVAIL myself of the time-honoured custom of a preface, not to make any reference or explanation concerning the "Symbols and Legends of Freemasonry"—if the book does not explain itself I have failed in my task and no preface can mend it—but as a means of expressing my gratitude to those gentlemen who have assisted and encouraged me in my work.

In the first place my thanks are most especially due to Mr. Walter Willis, A.K.C., Member Society of Engineers, from whose admirable etchings the illustrations to this book have been executed.

I also present my cordial thanks to Bros. Hughan, Simpson and Speth, for their careful revision of the text, and for many valuable suggestions, especially a suggestion from Bro. Speth, concerning the episode of Ben-hadad.

Lastly I record my hearty recognition of the encouragement and aid afforded me by the following eminent Brethren, through whose instigation and advice I was induced to publish this account of my studies of the truths and mysteries of our Craft :—Bros. W. Kelly (F.S.A., F.R.H.S.), P. Prov. G.M. and G. Supt. Leicester and Rutland ; S. S. Partridge, D.P.G.M. ; C. Henton Wood, P.P.S.G.W., Prov. G. Sec. ; J. T. Thorp, P.P.S.G.W., P.M. ; W. J. Freer, P.P.G.S.B., P.M. ; F. Griffith, P.P.G. Supt. of Works, P.M. 1265 ; F. Colman (F.C.A.), W.M. 1265 ; J. H. Thompson, P.P.S.G.D., P.M. 1265; Miles J. Walker, P.P.J.G.W., Prov. G.D.C., P.M. 1265 ; W. H. Goodwin, P.G.S.B., P.M. 1265 ; J. T. Harris, P.M. 1560.

THE AUTHOR.

TABLE OF CONTENTS.

	PAGES.
INTRODUCTORY.—Freemasonry Defined. The Sun in Splendour	1 to 3
INDIA.—Our Aryan Forefathers. The Triune God. Masonic Symbols	4 to 9
CHALDEA.—The land between two waters. The Hymn of Hea. The Antiquity of the Keystone. The False Arch. The True Arch. The Cube. The all-seeing Eye. A Grip or Token	9 to 17
EGYPT.—The Obscurity Beyond Knowledge. The Book of the Dead. Amen-Ra. Life, Death and Immortality. The Crux-Ansata. The Tau. The Stone Axe. The Cross. The Resurrection of the Dead. The Mystery of Death. The Great Legend of Antiquity. "I am, that I am." The Egyptian Mysteries. Masonic Clothing. Lodges of Instruction. Pyramid, Obelisk and Sphynx. The Square. The Level and the Keystone	17 to 37
JUDEA.—Biblical Masonry. The Tale of Two Brothers. Moses the great Law-giver. The Ark of Bulrushes. An Egyptian Romance. The Tabernacle and the Temple. History of the Canaanites. The Abominations of Babylon. Origin of the Etruscans. The Dionysiac Fraternity. Israel in the days of Solomon. The Temple of Solomon. The Idolatry of the Jews. The Building of the Temple. A sign or token in Holy Writ. The Essenes	37 to 72
GREECE.—The Immortality of the Soul. The Eleusinian Mysteries. The Greek Vases. The Rites of Eleusis. The Greater Mysteries. Pythagoras and Euclid	72 to 86

TABLE OF CONTENTS.

ITALY.—The Roman Colleges. The Foreign Influence of the Romans. Freemasonry in A.D. 79. A Masonic Lodge in Pompeii. The Christian Era. Christian Masonic Symbols. Masonry in the Middle Ages. The Freemasons of the Renaissance. The Mysteries of Rome ... 86 to 100

GERMANY.—The Scandinavian Legend. The Era of Charlemagne. The Steinmetzen. Origin of Gothic Architecture. Freemasons and the Romish Church ... ... 107 to 126

ENGLAND.—The Legacy of the Roman Masons. An Ancient Legend. Masons' Marks. Royal Masons. The English Tradition ... ... 126 to 145

MODERN FREEMASONRY.—The Last Great Link welded. The Constitution of 1723. The Compilation of the Ritual. Sneers of Sun Worship refuted. The Legend of Hiram Abif. Antiquity of the Legend. A Clue to its Origin. Solomon's Temple Exaggerated. The Battle of the Arches. Anderson as a Poet. Conclusion ... ... 145 to 164

LIST OF ILLUSTRATIONS,

Drawn by WALTER WILLIS, ESQ., A.K.C., *Member Society of Engineers, from original sketches, tracings, &c., by the Author.*

PLATE I., *page* 8.—*Fig.* 1. The Line which has neither End nor Beginning. 2. The Triangle. 3. Symbol on a Tomb 4 & 5. Symbols of Vishnu and Siva. 6. The Interlaced Triangles.

PLATE II., *page* 14.—*Fig.* 1. Ancient Arch at Abydos. 2. False Arch 3. Arch of the time of Abraham. 4. The Sacred Cube. 5. The All-seeing Eye. 6. Ancient Symbols. 7 A Grip or Token. 8. Ring of a Babylonian King.

PLATE III, *page* 18.—Arch in the Palace of Sargon at Khorsobad.

PLATE IV., *page* 24.—*Fig.* 1. The Promise of Immortality. 2. The Crux-Ansata. 3. The Tau. 4. The Symbols of Punishment. 5. Amen Ra. 6. An Egyptian Tombstone.

PLATE V., *page* 30.—*Fig.* 1. The Mysteries of Isis. 2. The Day of Judgment.

PLATE VI., *page* 36.—*Fig.* 1. Egyptian " Aprons." 2. Ministrant Priests. 3. Masonic Emblems from Pharaoh's Tomb. 4 A Keystone.

PLATE VII., *page* 56 —*Fig.* 1. Phœnician Tomb. 2. Etrurian Tomb. 3. An Etrurian Arch.

PLATE VIII., *page* 62.—*Fig.* 1. A Cyprian Coin. 2. Specimens of Egyptian Architecture. 3. Beam and Rest from the Temple at Karnac.

PLATE IX., *page* 80.—The Eleusinian Mysteries.

PLATE X., *page* 82.—*Fig.* 1. The Hierophant's Disk. 2. Greek Scale Plates. 3. Altar of Apollo.

PLATE XI., *page* 88.—*Figs.* 1 & 2. Masonic Stones in the Campidoglia Museum at Rome. 3. Tunisian Stele.

PLATE XII., *page* 94.—Mosaic from Pompeii.

PLATE XIII, *page* 100.—*Fig.* 1. Sketch from an old MS. 2. Church of St. Charles, Vienna.

PLATE XIV., *page* 106.—Masonic Emblems in Renaissance Pictures.

PLATE XV., *page* 122.—*Fig.* 1. Arch in Westminster Abbey. 2. Romanesque Arch. 3. Ancient "Greek Arch." 4. Masonic Alphabet.

This Account of the

Symbols and Legends of Freemasonry,

is Inscribed

To the

Worshipful Master, Officers, and Brethren of the Masonic Lodge, No. 2076,

known as

Quatuor Coronati,

As a humble tribute of my appreciation of their admirable and successful endeavours to dispel the clouds of doubt and the imputations of folly under which the Craft has so long suffered, and their efforts to place before the eyes of Students and Learned Men such an account of Freemasonry as is reasonable to common sense and in harmony with the ascertained facts of history.

J. Finlay Finlayson.

1st Jan., 1889.

THE SYMBOLS AND LEGENDS OF FREEMASONRY.

FREEMASONRY DEFINED.

FREEMASONRY is an institution of great antiquity, and is divided into two branches—operative and speculative.

The purport of operative Masonry has been to ameliorate the lot of man, and as far as possible to adorn his life with works of art and beauty.

Speculative Freemasonry teaches the existence of the Great Architect of the Universe, suggests the probability of an inner principle of life that survives the death of the body, and seeks to unite its members in the great brotherhood of man.

These doctrines are conveyed in symbols and legends. To trace the legends to their source and give some account of the history of the symbols is the aim proposed in these pages.

It must, however, be clearly understood by those who have not been initiated into the mysteries of Freemasonry, that no "open sesame" is offered for their acceptance, if they wish to know what is behind the veil they must seek that knowledge through the regular and legitimate channels. What is proposed for the uninitiated to obtain herein, is an acquaintance with the nature and historical truth of the great Masonic shrine wherein the wisdom of ages has handed down the effects of the wisest and best men of the world to solve the great problem of life, death, and a hereafter.

To the brethren of the Craft no apology is needed, they will see at a glance that the obligations of a Freemason have been faithfully maintained, and that scrupulous care has been taken to offer nothing connected with the science that is not already in print and open to the perusal of all. But, as may be readily admitted, among so numerous a body of men, a vast majority of Freemasons have neither the leisure nor the inclination to follow up these lines of study which are necessary for the full understanding of the symbols and legends of the Craft. A short digest of such study is here presented to them, giving a connected outline of the main points of interest and suggesting the roads which must be travelled over by those who are desirous of more extended information.

THE SUN IN SPLENDOUR.

The first great object that arrests the attention of the beholder on entering the Grand Lodge of Freemasons in London, is a large effigy of the Sun in splendour. It is placed directly above the throne on which the Grand Master of the Craft is seated when performing the functions of his exalted office.

Peering for some five or six thousand years down the long perspective of Time, as it narrows back toward the youth of the world, the disk of the life-giving sun, symbolising the sublime and incomprehensible Infinite, is the most prominent and tangible object that rises upon our view.

In these ever-recurring effigies the past and the present touch each other, the ancient and the modern beat together in one great unison of sympathy, and we see a vast chain of union starting out from the shadowy gloom of the antique world and pursuing its winding course till grasped in the living hand of to-day. The history of this chain is the history of Freemasonry. It is a record of an unceasing search for the author and guider of the Universe, it is the tablet whereon is written man's yearning for a future state in which he hopes that the perfect happiness he has conceived, but never attained, may be found.

To trace the intricate series of links composing this vast chain, and to catch the sympathetic harmonies they awaken, as they come ringing down the long avenues of the shifting ages, is the task immediately before us. It is to be pursued in Egypt, where first, with a light like that of the glow-worm, it sent its mild rays through the shadows of the old night of barbarism as they rolled away for the dawn of a new era. It is to be followed from the birthplace of our great Aryan forefathers to the banks of "the five rivers," to the smiling plains of fertile India. Its achievements must be read in Chaldea and Assyria, "the land between two waters." In Judea and in its marvellous book of Testimony. In Phœnicia, in Etruria, in Greece, in Rome, in Carthage. In renaissant Italy, through the monasteries and the mediæval guilds, through the glories of the Cathedrals, through the works of the steinmetzen of Germany, and the apprentices and craftsmen of our own land, till its vestiges appear joined together in harmony and still working unceasingly for the good of mankind in the Speculative Freemasonry of to-day.

INDIA.

OUR ARYAN FOREFATHERS.

Let us first direct our attention to that great race whose primæval home was the widespread highland plateau to the north of the Hindu-Kush. The Aryan, the "noble race" as they called themselves, from whom we Anglo-Saxons trace a direct descent. A race whose origin is so remote and of such traditionary antiquity that it is by no means impossible that they may have been the primary source of those other marvellous races, the Hamitic and the Semitic, on whose greatness the whole foundation of our modern civilisation rests.

The history of the world has one specially marked feature written upon it—the record of those great race movements which we call emigrations. The tracing out of these movements and the consequences attendant upon them compose one of the leading aims of the historian.

Of the first great emigration, the settlement of Egypt by the Hamitic race, no record nor trace of a record is left. Six thousand years ago that wonderful race was already upon the banks of the Nile and had already brought the arts and sciences into a high state of cultivation.

The second great emigration was that of the Aryans into India, which occurred not less than four thousand years ago. Two other emigrations in which branches of the same stock were concerned, have produced such momentous results on the civilisation of the world, that a short notice of them may be advantageously introduced. The first of them, which like a great tidal wave, swept across the decaying civilisations of Rome and

Athens, ultimately peopled Germany, France, Spain, Northern Italy, and Great Britain, with those intelligent inhabitants by whom our modern civilisation has been developed. The second is the great emigration to the New World, still incompleted, still in the cradle of its infancy, giving as yet but faint prophecies of the stupendous world changes which its manhood is in all probability destined to achieve.

As this last emigration rode over and subjugated the ignorant Red Man, the Blacks, and the Maori, so did the great Aryan emigration despise and control the aboriginals of India, founding over the ruins of their degradation and barbarism an empire whose annals present an unbroken sequence of the sweetest thoughts and the noblest imaginings the mind of man has ever conceived.

To fix the date of this emigration is beyond the power of research. We know that over two thousand years before Christ bands of pastoral and agricultural tribes left their homes in Iran or Bactria, crossed the great Hindu-Kush and settled on the banks of the five rivers of the Punjaub. By tradition we know that these new comers into India were a peaceful, single-minded people, virtuous in their lives and seekers after the sublime truths of the infinite. The sun, the moon, fire, and whatever was striking and beautiful in nature commanded their admiration and adoration, as these spoke in their glory and in their beauty of the omniscient power reflected through them.

After many years had elapsed, after the old Aryan tongue had developed into the Sanscrit, the first of the great Hindu scriptures intended as a guide of life, the Vedas, made their appearance in the world. They are four in number, and are a collection of prayers, hymns, and rubrics. The most ancient and the most beautiful is that called the Rig Veda. Our earliest touch of this antique work goes back to not less than fifteen hundred years before the Christian era. It breathes throughout a free and natural feeling, a yearning for the truth of the infinite, and a warm love for the beauties of nature.

Its priests and teachers were the Brahmins. They taught the people that there is but one God, and they called their god Brahm—"the one eternal mind, the self-existing incomprehensible spirit." "He whom the mind alone can perceive." "That which cannot be personified." The symbol through which they led their minds to contemplate this wondrous mystery was expressed by the outline of a circle which was intended to represent the sun. The meaning the sun conveyed to these early Hindus is clearly expressed in the following verse of the Rig Veda, the Gayatri, the most sacred verse, which every Brahmin repeats to this day in his devotions morning and evening, as Christian rubrics repeat the Lord's prayer.

"We meditate on that excellent light of the divine Sun; may he illuminate our minds."

Later on the same beautiful thought is again eloquently expressed in the pages of the Atharva Veda.

"Thou, O God, goest mightily across the earth.

"Thou sittest brilliantly on the altar at the sacrifice.

"The Prophets carry thee as a purifier.

"Purify us from all misdeeds."

Here, then, we have the disk of the Sun exhibited as the first link of a chain in which the Sun in Splendour in the Masonic Lodges of to-day is the latest manifestation.

THE TRIUNE GOD.

But the Brahmins, while teaching the oneness of Brahm, never lost sight of those attributes of greatness through which the operations of his works present themselves to the understanding of man. To these, the great forces of fire and water, they gave the names of Vishnu and Siva, forming, with Brahma, the great Hindu Trinity, a mystery which the celebrated Hindu poet, Kalidâsa, translated by Griffith, has described in terms bearing remarkable resemblance to the well-known words of the Athanasian creed.

" In those three Persons the one God was shown.

" Each first in place, each last —not one alone was known.

" Of Siva, Vishnu, Brahma, each may be

" First, second, third, among the blessed three."

With the advance of time the study of the arts and sciences had so prospered with those early pioneers of civilisation that at least the elements of geometry were known to them. It is, therefore, not surprising to find that the symbols of the Hindu pantheon were geometric in form and that they described through geometric demonstrations the attributes they were proposed to present.

In this higher development the disk (*Fig. 1, Plate* I.) does something more than represent the physical face of the Sun. Its circumference, a line which has neither end nor beginning, most clearly represents the great attributes of the Eternal. The point in the centre, called Purm, is the inner essence of Brahm, from which all emanates and around which all revolves.

Still progressing in their studies, the equilateral Triangle, Trikum (*Fig. 2, Plate* I.), takes its place among the symbols, and represents Brahma, the Triune God, with his visible attendants, Vishnu (water) and Siva (fire).

The triangle, with its point turned uppermost, as flames dart upward to the sky, denotes Siva, the spirit of fire.

The triangle, with its point turned downward, as the rain falls down from heaven, denotes Vishnu, the spirit of water.

Two triangles interlaced, called Sherkum (*Fig.* 6, *Plate* I.), represent Vishnu and Siva. The elements of fire and water.

A circle with an upward pointing triangle (*Fig.* 4 and 5, *Plate* I.) represents the spirit of fire acting by the direction of the eternal.

A circle within a downward pointing triangle represents, in like manner, the guided spirit of water.

The symbol (*Fig.* 3, *Plate* I.) is to be found everywhere in the ancient monuments of India. Among the many instances recorded the two following may be referred to. The interlaced triangles with the dot, Purm, is to be seen most conspicuously at Delhi on the tomb of a Mahommedan, Humayun, the Mogul Emperor, the father of Akbar. It may also be seen sculptured on a very large scale on each side of the gateway of the fort of Agra.

With these symbols to contemplate no Freemason need be reminded of the position of the square and compasses as they are seen on the volume of Holy Writ when the Lodge is duly open. With what new force will they not cause him to recall the words of the rubric:—"The jewel of the Royal Arch is a double triangle within a circle of gold. The intersecting

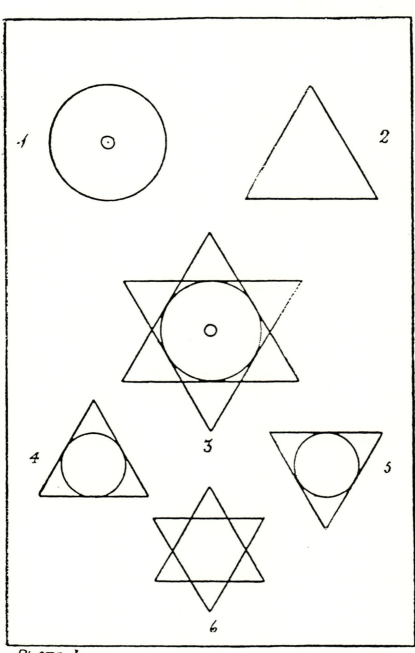

PLATE. I.

triangles denote the elements of fire and water, the sun in the centre with its diverging rays is an emblem of the Deity. The encircling ring is an emblem of eternity and infinity."

CHALDEA.
THE LAND BETWEEN TWO WATERS.

As might be expected, the vast emigrations of the ancient days, to which reference has been made, were directed to the rich alluvial soils that bordered the great and never-failing rivers. The five rivers of the Punjaub, and afterwards the Ganges, provided hospitable welcome to the Aryan founders of India. The seemingly endless length of the fertile shores of the Yang-tse-kiang drew forth the great Tauranian emigration and gave birth to the ancient empire of China. The rich lands around the Euphrates and the Tigris attracted an emigration of the semetic races that built up the marvellous cities of Babylon and Nineveh. And, above all—the Nile, whose never-failing floods gave home and life to the earliest of all emigrations, that of the great Hamitic people, the Egyptians, the most learned, and the most remarkable race that the old time produced.

Let us see what record concerning Masonry the Euphrates and the Tigris have to offer us through the land of Mesopotamia, in the glorious cities of Babylon and Nineveh.

There in the twilight of the ages the first ray that illuminates our vision and brings us a knowledge of the past comes again from the symbolic disk of the sun. In those ancient cuneiform inscriptions cut into bricks of baked clay, a collection of which is treasured up in the cases of the British Museum, we find a continuous story that makes the old time night to glow with the vividness of the day. To what early period of history these baked bricks may be referred, no man can tell. They are older than Babylon itself, and Babylon is the accepted name of the ancient Babel of Scripture.

The inscriptions are in Akkad, the language of the aboriginal inhabitants who preceded the Chaldeans, written, without the shadow of a doubt, centuries upon centuries before the days of Moses. Some of the inscriptions are in both Akkad and Chaldean, a fact which goes far to show that the legends and myths of their forerunners were accepted by the Magi of Chaldea.

The following excerpt, taken from Fox-Talbot's "Records of the Past," is a translation of the hymn of Hea, God of the Ocean, the Akkadian equivalent of Vishnu, the anti-type of Neptune :—

"In my right hand I hold my fiery disk.

"In my left hand I hold my murderous disk.

"The sun with fifty faces, the upraised weapon of my divinity, I hold it.

"The valiant one who breaks the mountains, the sun whose influence none can escape, I hold it.

"The burning God of the East, who makes his glory shine like that of the day, I hold him."

Here indeed is a vivid picture both of the disk of the sun and the sun in splendour :—the sun with fifty faces ; the weapon of divinity ; the rayed or flaming sun ; the Tchakra or wheel of Buddha ; the mystical disk of Brahma ; the Crux Ansata of Amen Ra ; the weapon of the Cherubim ; the flaming sword which turned every way to keep the way of the tree of life ; the Shekinah ; the flame of fire out the midst of a bush, in which symbol Moses saw the God of Israel face to face:—the sun in splendour that adorns and glorifies the Masonic Lodge.

It was in such vivid words as the following that those early dwellers in Mesopotamia recorded their belief in the personality of the sun.

"Sun from the foundations of heaven thou art risen.
"Thou hast unfastened the bolts of the shining skies.
"Thou hast opened the door of heaven."

To what high perfection their Semitic successors pushed the grand legacies this wonderful race left behind is proved by the marvellous record of Chaldean Astronomy. The clay tablets, dating from at least twenty centuries before Christ, contain a complete account of their researches and understanding of Mathematics, Geography, Grammar, and Mythology. Moreover, it is here in Mesopotamia that we first find the fullest development of the Arch. It is true that the arch, both with and without the keystone, the false arch and the true arch, was known at least contemporaneously in Egypt, but the Egyptians commonly made the arch of only subdominant importance in their architecture, while the Chaldeans and the Assyrians made it the main and constant feature of their structures.

THE ANTIQUITY OF THE KEYSTONE.

Let us trace the circumstances that gave birth to a demand in Mesopotamia for the services of the arch.

It is well known that the fertility of these lands of scant rainfall and frequent drought was ensured by vast works of irrigation. The Euphrates and the Tigris provided the life-giving fluid abundantly, but it needed the skilled hand of man to spread the water over the sun-parched land and parcel it out among cultured fields far away from the parent stream.

Such works were considered to shed the highest lustre on the rulers and potentates of those dominions. The great dam across the Tigris below Mosul, which diverts the waters of that river, was built by the "mighty hunter," and is to this day called "Sahr-el-Nimrud." Here, in further evidence, is a translation of an unspeakably ancient inscription—

"The canal Khammurabi, the joy of man, a stream of abundant waters for the people of Sumir and Akkad I excavated. Its banks, all of them I restored to newness, new supporting walls I heaped up. Perennial waters for the people of Sumir and Akkad I provided."

Is it not easy to see that here comes the great demand for the arch? To carry on extensive irrigation works and canals, even in a country of wide extended plains, aqueducts must have been called for. This the text of the above quoted inscription itself tells clearly—" Its banks, all of them I restored to newness, new supporting walls I heaped up." What are these heaped up walls but the forerunners of the aqueduct on arches, the ruins of which still dot the solitudes of the Orient, and whose descendants, like grim vestiges of the past, yet remain and add their weird, though picturesque charm to the oppressive stillness of the Roman compagna.

Even historians of the later ages give Babylon full credit for the arch. Strabo and Diodorus both say the arch was known to the Chaldeans, and that the famous hanging gardens of Babylon were supported on the true arch.

But we have yet further proof than that of history to convince us of the great antiquity and early perfection of the arch. The ruins of vaulted works of the most ancient construction are still to be found. The great French orientalist, Mariette, tells us that the arch of a tomb at Abydos dates as far back as the sixteenth dynasty, a period of at least eighteen centuries before the Christian era.

The city of Abydos was one of the earliest cities of Egypt and celebrated for the worship of Osiris. As will be seen by the illustration (*Fig.* 1, *Plate* II), the keystone, the all-important principle of the true arch, was perfectly well known to the Egyptians at a very early period of their history. But specimens of such nature, forming an important feature in architectural structures, are not common in Egypt, and it is to Babylon and Nineveh that we must turn when we seek frequent illustration of the fully utilised principle.

The building material of those cities was for the most part bricks of baked or sun-dried clay, not unlike the *adobe* used in Mexico and Southern California to this day. They were stuck together with a slimy earth of which frequent mention may be found in the Bible. "And they had brick for stone, and slime had they for mortar."—Genesis xi., 3. Stone was not uncommon in the Royal buildings, but as stone of sufficient hardness is not found in the valley of the Euphrates it had to be transported thither at considerable cost from a distance. Brick set in bitumen or asphalt, drawn from the pits at Hit on the Euphrates, was therefore adopted as its substitute, and, as the ruins at Ur (Mughier) and of the magnificent palace of Sargon at Khorsobad still show, answered its purpose admirably.

In Egypt, where stone was more readily obtainable, the false or set-off arch (*Fig.* 2, *Plate* II.) was not of infrequent use. But it never attained to any large dimensions and was seldom used for any higher purpose than a subway for carrying off rainfall and superfluous waters from the courts and terraces of the palaces.

To chip the under surfaces of blocks of stone was an easy proceeding, but to contrive a false arch of brick called for considerable ingenuity. (*Fig.* 3, *Plate* II.) representing the portal of a tomb chamber at Mughier, gives a ready illustration of the method employed in Chaldea and Assyria. The great antiquity thus presented may be realised by calling back to mind that Mughier is the ancient Ur, where lived Terah, ninth in descent from Noah. "And Terah took Abram, his son, and Lot, the son of Haran, his son's son, and Sarai, his daughter-in-law, his son Abram's wife, and they went forth with them from Ur of the Chaldees to go into the land of Canaan."—Genesis xi., 31.

But while the set-off arch continued to find some favour for commoner or domestic purposes, the true arch took its place in all the sumptuous palaces of the great Kings of the East. The accompanying illustration (*Plate* III., *Page* 18) of an arch and court in the harem of the vast and magnificent palace of Sargon, at Khorsobad, taken from Place's "Ninive," gives some idea of the position the arch and the vault occupied in the architecture of the two great nations of Mesopotamia.

It is not necessary to apologize to a Freemason for an extended notice of the arch. The secret of King Solomon, of Hiram, King of Tyre, and of Hiram Abif, occupies so important a place in Masonry that too much

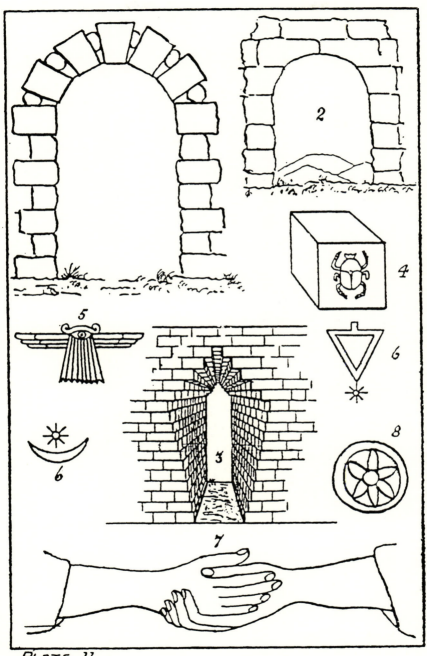

PLATE. II.

attention cannot be given to the subject. To prove the antiquity of the arch and a knowledge of the keystone prior to the building of King Solomon's Temple is a matter of no small importance. But till very late years accepted authorities, men of such standing as Ottofried Müller held that the most ancient arch in the world was the Cloaca Maxima, which to this day exists almost intact beneath the ruins of the Forum of ancient Rome. Had it been true that the arch had no existence before the early times of Rome, the Masonic account of the Temple Arch would have been foundationless; but its antiquity having been proved beyond even the possibility of a doubt, an internal evidence is given to the Masonic legend that sheds a new lustre and adds additional probability to the truth of the ancient traditions of the Craft.

A more extended notice of the builders of this great Roman sewer, and the possibility of their connection with the building of King Solomon's temple, will be given when treating of the arts of Etruria.

To those who desire to further follow up the emblems of Masonry in Mesopotamia and its vicinity, most interesting information will be found in C. W. King's " Antique Gems and Rings," Layard's " Nineveh and Babylon," in Place's " Ninive," and in the valuable publications of the " Palestine Exploration Fund." The accompanying examples of Masonic symbols are among the many that may be found in their pages.

The cube (*Fig.* 4, *Plate* II.) was from the earliest times a venerated symbol, and the double cube, " the oblong square" of Masonry, signified immensity of space " from the foundations of the earth to the zenith of the heavens." The cube was the sacred emblem of the Lydian Kubele, known to Rome in after ages as Ceres or Cybele. The derivation of the word "cube" from its ancient signification is clearly apparent.

The "all-seeing eye" (*Fig.* 5, *Plate* II.) is from an ancient Assyrian cylinder, in which it appears placed prominently above an altar whereon a King is offering sacrifice.

Masonic symbols (*Fig.* 6, *Plate* II.) are from a Babylonian cylinder or seal, composed of iron hematite, and are placed over the sacrifice of a bull.

A GRIP OR TOKEN.

Among the wealth of treasures to be seen in the Louvre are some half-dozen headless statues from Chaldea of the most remote antiquity. They are cut in a very hard dark greenish-coloured igneous rock, which must have been transported to Babylon from a great distance. Some of these statues are seated and some are standing upright. A collection of heads, evidently broken off other statues of like nature, is also exhibited, and is of very high value in shewing the race and character of these people.

The statues are without doubt those of great Kings. The costliness of the material, and the vast labour of working it in consequence of the hardness of the stone, the high finish and the minute attention to detail, bear in themselves this testimony. Stately, grand immovable, and patient, they stood in the temples of their God, waiting, as the centuries roll by, in the calmness of peace and the confidence of surety, their great awakening in a new and glorified day.

One remarkable peculiarity is to be found in each of the statues. The hands pressed close to the breast and clasped, as we see in the illustration (*Fig. 7, Plate* II.). We learn from ancient histories that the ancient kings went through initiations into the mysteries of the god they worshipped, and had doubtless secret means of communication with each other, and of making known their election in the faith. The Rev. J. Milner, in his remarkable address on " Freemasonry Older than the Ancient Mysteries," says :— " Even those who had been initiated into the Eleusinian mysteries had something corresponding to the " Masonic Grip," as may be read in " Epihanus." Such being the case, may we not fairly conclude that the attitude of these statues bears evident intention of hands prepared for a " grip or token," which at the great day of revivification would give them a right to take their place with the elect, and pass them on to the life beyond. A personal experiment will at once show that the clasped hands is by no means the result of a natural position, to place them in the position indicated is clearly an effort of forethought and intention.

EGYPT.

THE OBSCURITY BEYOND KNOWLEDGE.

Egypt, the land of wonders, the birthplace of the sciences, the nurse of the arts, and the mother of truth, is a mighty name that impresses alike both the unlearned and the student. The Biblical narrative has indelibly impressed on us all its antiquity, its learning, and its grandeur. But with what greater force do not those facts come home to us in these later days, since the genius of Champollion has deciphered the language of the hieroglyphics, and given our learned men a means wherewith they can place before us the very language, the actual words, of records written six thousand years ago.

Do they teach us of Masonry? Let us judge.

First of all they teach us of the existence of the one God, the creator of heaven and earth. The priests, the select men, the depository of all learning, the guiders and councillors of the king had no doubt as to a prime originating cause. They named it Ptah—"The obscurity beyond knowledge." As unknown then as now. As unteachable in the early days of Egypt as it is at the present period.

On these men devolved the duty of welding into harmony the conflicting passions and the varying needs of the vast masses of mankind. Kings and rulers may represent the terrors of physical force, the spear, the arrow and the whip. But these are but men whom the arrow can transfix and the pestilence lay low. They may bend men's backs beneath the lash and force them to the task, but they cannot bind their hearts into one enthusiastic whole, worshipping at once with love and awe that irresistible unseen and imperishable force that is felt alike in the blaze of the sun, the rushing of the wind, and the ceaseless flow of the waters. To personify this power was the task of the priests.

Ptah, in Egyptian, signifies architect, former, conductor—the "Architect of the Universe," "The God who made himself to be God," "The double being," "The begetter of the first beginning," "The creator of heaven and earth who has made all things, the Lord of all that is and is not." Such was the description the Egyptian priests would give of the Lord of Lords. But

PLATE III

this God was a God at once too sublime and too shadowy to be grasped by the minds of the ignorant and lowly men of those days. They must have something tangible, something that had a self-contained proof of its irresistible and all-pervading might. What more irresistible, what more all-pervading than the Sun? called in the Egyptian by the name of RA. Plutarch tells us that the Egyptians—"regard the Sun as the body of the beneficent power, the visible form of a being only comprehensible to thought."

Here, then, was the foundation—a being only comprehensible to thought must have some name which common men shall know him by, in which they shall express their dread of his terrors, and their gratitude for the bounties they receive at his hands. Hence the first stage is achieved—"the soul of the sun"—RA—is the name by which men's tongues shall greet him. Thus is he described in the early church of Egypt, in that wonderful book, the "Ritual of the Dead," or as it might still more aptly be termed, the Book of the Resurrection.

"Hail, thou who comest as Ptah and who hast been the creator of the Gods.

"Hail, thou who hast come as the soul of the holy souls in Amenti.

"Hail, thou who comest in radiance and travellest in thy disk.

"Hail, among the Gods, weigher of words in the kingdom of the dead.

"Hail, thou hast slain the guilty, thou hast destroyed the spirit of darkness."

Pure and beautiful as is the spirit breathed forth in these words, they still breathed of heights too serene and of depths too profound for the work-a-day heart of man to soar or to fathom. The symbol must be nearer to the touch, the outer eye must see it as the inner senses feel it. Man, or the image of man, must be clothed with the attributes of God, something of wood or stone, in which superstition may set the "dread and awe" of things, and before which the untaught multitude may kneel and grovel in the dust.

Here, then, we have the initiation of the Pantheon of Egypt. A statue is presented to the people, his name is Amen-Ra (*Fig.* 5, *Plate* iv.) RA—the Sun, AMEN—the concealed, or veiled one. He is seated on a throne, in his right hand is the Crux-ansata, the ring-handled cross, the emblem of divine life. In his left hand he holds the sceptre, symbol of purity of life, surmounted by an effigy of the bird called koucoupha, symbol of divine beneficence. RA is he, the eternal, the life giver: AMEN, the concealed, or hidden one. Veiled in allegory and illustrated in symbol. The great god of Egypt, Amen-Ra, in whom, and through whom all things exist.

LIFE, DEATH, AND IMMORTALITY.

What do Masons find concealed in the allegory, and illustrated in the symbol? "In his right hand the crux-ansata (*Fig.* 2, *Plate* iv.) the ringed cross, the emblem of divine life." The disk of the sun at once presents itself, again the great genealogy is before us. Through India, through Chaldea, through the Bible, through Egypt, down to the sun in splendour that beams above the Master's chair. Crux-ansata is the name by which western nations have known this symbol, while, in the hands of monarchs, of their own lands, it still appears as cross and orb. Ank was its Egyptian name; its power, in the writing of the hieroglyphics, in which it frequently appears, is equivalent to the word life. As a symbol in the hand of Amen-Ra, it means still more, it means earthly life, with its trials and punishments, and the eternity of life to come.

Around the disk of the sun is the ring that ends not, nor begins, the type of eternity : beneath it two lines symbolical of the two lands, the earth below and the heavens above (*Fig.* 1, *Plate* iv.).

A still further signification attaches itself to the ring. In the majority of instances the ring is elongated, giving it somewhat of an egg-shaped appearance. This is typical of the ancient belief that all nature sprung from an egg. In the opening line of Paradise Lost, " When thou sat'st, dove-like, brooding o'er the vast abyss," Milton expresses the same idea. We read in the Egyptian Book of the Dead,—" Oh, sun in his egg, shining from his horizon, floating in the clouds, without an equal among the gods." And again,—" I shine as the egg which is in the hidden region." There can be no doubt but that this ancient myth is one, and by no means the least of the veiled traditions locked up in the mysterious Crux-Ansata.

Divested of the ring, we have that great Masonic symbol, the Tau (*Fig.* 3, *Plate* iv.), which, here, has its origin and its true form, the real meaning of which the hieroglyphic writings will teach us.

The hieroglyphic sign for the word God is an axe. Moreover, the axe represented is a "stone axe," bearing in itself peculiar testimony to the great antiquity of the symbol, and to the fact that dread, terror, and punishment were chief among the earliest attributes the mind of man associated with the Deity.

We have here the symbol writing, by which the words "afflict or punish" are represented.

The word "revenge" is thus depicted in hieroglyphics. On the left are the parallel lines above a circle, denoting the lord of two worlds; beneath them, the upper half of a hemisphere, typifying the heavens, in the centre is the cross or gallows; to the left is a palm leaf, a sign used to designate the earth. These are the attributes of the God of heaven and earth, who, from the heavens, punishes the evil doers of the earth. "Vengeance is mine, saith the Lord, I will repay."

The symbol of revenge, though always maintaining the original conception, varies sometimes in its form, and takes the following shapes—(*Fig.* 4, *Plate* iv.), some of which we shall meet in startling significance in other lands, divided in time by thousands of years, but alike identical in their signification.

The reference which has already been made to the "Book of the dead," written in all probability not less than 6000 years ago, will point out the sanctity in which the fact of death was held by the Egyptians, and from it may be surmised the hope of immortality, which, we shall find, was the underlying strength of the Egyptian faith. This firm hope and belief we first find clearly written on the tombstones of the dead.

THE RESURRECTION OF THE DEAD.

The accompanying sketch from a tombstone—shown in the rich Egyptian exhibit in the Louvre, (*Fig.* 6, *Plate* iv.)—was a stereotyped form in use throughout the temples of sepulture in ancient Egypt. The tombstones look to the east, whence the final day of triumph will spring upon the world. The two eyes of the Sun guard north and south all harm which might assail the body of the dead during his sojourn in the west, where his actions and words have been weighed in the balance of the judge. Beneath all is the ring cross—shorn of its terrors. The Tau no more holds him subject to its dreaded pains. The promise of eternity, the life in both worlds is assured to him.

Nor was this glorious hope taught alone in the concealment of an allegory and the illustration of a symbol. The following excerpt, taken from "Egypt under the Pharaohs," by H. Brugsch-Bey, is a translation of a hymn to the sun, written in the reign of Amenhotep IV., 1466 B.C. :—

"Beautiful is thy setting, thou sun's disk of life,
"Thou Lord of Lords and King of the worlds,
"Thou O God who art in truth the living one, standest before the two eyes,
"Thou art he which created what never was, which formest everything that is in the universe."

The yearning of man for that completed happiness which shone like a glory before him in the aspirations of his heart, but vanished away and faded into darkness as he approached the goal, was ever seeking a solution of the problem, and ever peering for a hidden road which might lead him to a condition so longed for, but so long sought in vain. Great nature, RA himself, gave the solution and lighted up the road. The first pledge of renewal after death was discovered in what men saw happen to the sun every day and every year. He, too, died, and he revived. And was he not a living being? Had he not become a personal deity? Were not men his children?

Such was the Hindu belief in immortality, and the hope of life to come was in no other people more deeply rooted than in the Egyptians. In Cher-nuter, the divine under-world, the sinner must be judged. Like the sun, all must die and enter the kingdom of the west, then they who while they lived on earth had trod in the path of virtue, and whose words were not found wanting, would rise again with Osiris in the east and reign with him in the abodes of light.

The resurrection of the dead thus taught was not only the resurrection of the purified spirit; it went further, it taught the resurrection of the body. The following hymn is translated by Dr. Birch, of the British Museum, from a papyrus, dating not less than 2500 B.C.—

"O sun, under thy name of RA., when thou openest the secret places in the gate of Amenti, the place of departed spirits, rejoicing the hearts of the gods, restore to me my heart, for I am a perfected spirit.

"Thou art sure, I am saved, *as thy limbs* are sound, so are *my limbs* sound."

THE MYSTERY OF DEATH.

But it is not Masonic symbolism alone that is to be found in the history and monuments of ancient Egypt, something of far greater importance, lying at the very root of Masonic teaching, is enshrined in this great testimony of the past. All writers and all peoples of the world saw and comprehended the fact that everywhere around them nature died, and, after a period of rest, rose again with renewed vigour and commenced afresh a course of life. The sun sunk at night into the portals of the west, and darkness overshadowed the earth; but in the morning with new brightness, with regenerated

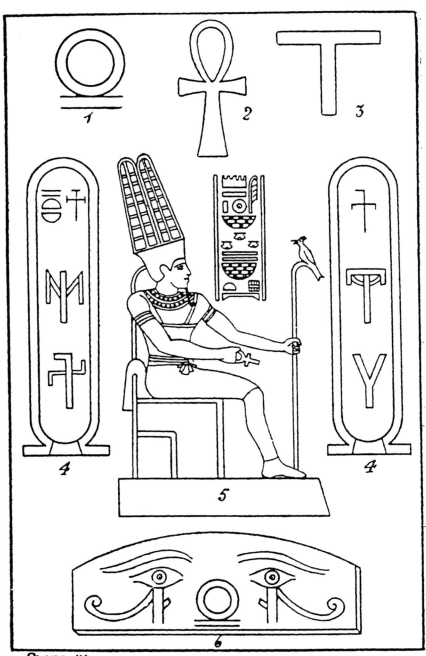

PLATE. IV.

strength, he climbed the steep vault of the heavens and lighted up the world with the effulgence of his glory. Each year as the sadness of the autumn brought the falling Equinox, his vigour languished, and the once all-pervading sun fell a weakling into the cold lap of the winter solstice. But as the three months that assailed him and the three months that sought in vain to hold him, passed on in the never-ending circle of the years, his beauty and his beneficence returned to him, till at last he mounted in triumph to the blazing constellation of Leo and his empire was again exultant on the earth.

The leaves fell and withered into dust, but the spring brought new leaves and expanded into fresh forms of loveliness. Man died, his ashes were gathered by pious hands, swathed in cere clothes to keep them from the decaying influences of the pernicious air, anointed with cunning drugs so as to bid defiance alike to the perishing finger of time and the foul ravages of the worm. Guarded with jealous care, watched with affectionate regard, though in the silence of the tomb, esteemed, not dead, but living, like the falling sun, like last year's leaves, awaiting only the grand vernal equinox, when the eastern doors of his long habitation should burst open and the dead should rise triumphantly into the kingdoms of immortality and unto life made perfect.

The Brahmins in the mysterious depths of their cavern temples, performed rites and ceremonies wherein these great facts were enshrined and typified. The Chaldean legend of the descent of Istar into Hades, and its kindred stories were each but fresh versions of nature's history through life, death and regeneration, and are without doubt the fathers of that great legend which forms the central feature, the pith and life of Freemasonry.

If we would clearly understand the allegory contained in the death of Hiram Abif we must seek it in Egypt in the rites and mysteries of Osiris, for there, as may be satisfactorily shown, is the true source of the great Masonic legend.

THE GREAT LEGEND OF ANTIQUITY.

Of very ancient origin indeed is the legend on which the Osiric myth is based. Six thousand years ago, Osiris was the god, the great personification of the sun, whom all Egypt worshipped and flocked in on every side to adore in his temple at Abydos. Isis, his consort, the moon, the all-mother, the Queen of Heaven, and Horus, their son, formed a triune god, which later ranked in men's minds in manner with the Brahm, Vishnu, and Siva of India. Osiris, who had come as a mortal on earth to ameliorate and soften the lot of man, reigned as King over Egypt. Being desirous of spreading the benefits of his civilisation to other nations he left the care of his throne to his wife, Queen Isis. During his absence his brother, Typhon, wrought a conspiracy against him. On the return of Osiris, Typhon, in the month of November, invited him to a banquet to be held in his honour. At the banquet Typhon produced a chest or ark painted with beautiful designs and inlaid with gold, promising to give it to any person whose body it would fit. Osiris unsuspectingly laid himself down in the chest, when the lid was immediately closed over him, fastened down, and the ark cast into the Nile.

The body of Osiris was for a long time tossed about on the waves of the sea, till at last it was cast up at

Byblos, in Phœnicia, and embedded amid the branches of a tamarisk tree. Isis, with great lamentation, sought her husband throughout the world, braving fearful dangers among rugged rocks, sterile lands and darkness, till at last the moon came to her rescue and guided her to the tamarisk tree whose sheltering branches waved over the precious ark. She bore the body home to Egypt, and with great pomp and ceremony committed it to the tomb. Meanwhile, Horus, horrified at the treachery of his uncle, Typhon, immediately slew him, and, having ascended the throne, proceeded to his father's tomb and there brought him back to life.

Such, though it is told with endless variation, is the outline of the legend of Osiris, and on this the mysteries of Egypt were based. The change of the seasons, the alternations of day and night, the assistant light of the changeful moon, the recurrence of drought, of pestilence and famine, the ever presence of death, and the regeneration of matter, each testifying to some great and all-powerful agent lying in the "Obscurity beyond knowledge." This is what may be called the plot of the great drama of the mysteries. The priests were well aware that in knowing these things they knew all that man can know, and, at the same time, clearly perceived that their knowledge was nought. But priestcraft had to be maintained ; what was knowledge in the mind of the untiring student of the truth, was blasphemy to the uninitiated. To govern the people, a direct and visible power must be bodily before them. The mysteries supplied the want. To those who could read beyond the veil, there lie the unerring truth ; but to the great mass of mankind the outer shell, the physical drama enacted before them, was all they asked or wanted, or, indeed, could comprehend.

The Greeks sought to dive beneath the surface, but the wily Egyptian priests took refuge in the obscurity of their sanctuaries, and met such enquirers as Plato, Pythagoras, Herodotus, and Solon, who interrogated them of their mysteries, and sought to be inducted into their rites, with such baffling enigma as the following:—

"I am that I am ; I am all that has been, and all that will be, and no man has lifted the veil that covers me."

Plutarch tells us that when the sun was in Scorpio, in the month of Athyr, the Egyptians enclosed the body of their God Osiris in an ark or chest, and that, during this ceremony, a great annual festival was celebrated. Three days after the priests had enclosed Osiris, they gave out that they had found him again, and the people went down to the river, shouting—"Osiris is found." The death of Osiris was lamented when the sun was in Scorpio ; he then descended into the lower hemisphere ; but when he rose again, at the vernal equinox, then Osiris was said to be born anew.

Herodotus, speaking of the lake at Sais, says : "On this lake it is that the Egyptians represented by night his sufferings I refrain from mentioning, and these representations they call their Mysteries. I know well the whole course of the proceedings in these ceremonies, but they shall not pass my lips."

The Honble. W. C. Stuart, whose interesting books, "Gleanings of the Nile" and the "Text of an Egyptian Queen," contain much valuable information, tells us that the legend of Osiris and Isis forms the illustration of the roof paintings of the Temple of Dendera. He also tells us that what he considered Masonic emblems were frequently met with in his travellings on the Nile.

One instance he records of two pillars placed side by side with a blazing sun immediately above and between them. It is greatly to be regretted that in both instances the author did not find it desirable to afford us further information on so interesting a subject.

The accompanying sketch (*Fig.* 1, *Plate* v.), which is taken from "Stellar and Masonic Astronomy," by R. H. Brown, is said to be copied from the sarcophagus of a king, and is an illustration of the very highest interest. It would have been desirable to have been furnished with some fuller description of its origin than "the sarcophagus of a king," but the sketch, rough as it is, contains sufficient intrinsic evidence of its genuineness to enable us to receive it as a valuable contribution to Osiac research. It represents in all probability the initiation of a king into the mysteries of Isis. He has evidently passed through such a tragic end as that of our Grand Master, Hiram Abif, and the Lion by the secret grip and the Crux-ansata, the token of everlasting life, is about to raise the royal candidate from his figurative tomb. Meanwhile, Isis standing before the altar and using the words recorded in the papyrus found in the ruins of Thebes, rejoices at the emblematic return of Osiris the Sun.

"Hail to thee, thou divine Lord.
"There is no God like unto Thee,
"Heaven hath thy Soul,
"Earth hath thy remains,
"The lower heaven is in possession of thy mysteries."

In testimony of the value of this illustration it may be said that the headdress and attitude of Isis and the fact of her being present as a priestess at the initiation are in every way correct. Mariette, the highest and most reliable authority on Egyptian matters, gives us a picture in his album of the Boulak museum, wherein a king appears before the judgment seat of Osiris, and behind him stands a representation of Isis, identical in attitude and clothing with that which appears in Mr. Brown's illustration (*Fig.* 2, *Plate* v.) That a representative of Isis took part in the celebration of the mysteries is a fact recorded by Apuleius.

It will be noticed that the return of the sun to the fulness of his glory is typified in Leo, and not in Cancer, according to the present position of the summer solstice in the Zodiac. But it must be remembered that this difference is easily to be accounted for by the procession of the equinoxes. The orbit in which the earth completes its passage round the sun is a vast spiral, commencing beyond the most distant planets with a diameter many multiples of its present diameter, and dwindling down till the completion of time shall have reduced it to its absorption in the sun. Thus it is evident, as the track becomes shorter and shorter every year, the arrival of the earth at a given point on the Zodiac is in equal manner accelerated, and the summer solstice, which once presented itself in the constellation of Leo, now appears by anticipation in that of its neighbour Cancer (*See Appendix, page* i.)

That this change has actually taken place we have abundant contemporary testimony. In the ritual of the " Book of the Dead " we find the following :—

" Lord of the earth in a box is thy name."

" All the Gods to the utmost are humiliated at the words of the Lord of the Chest."

" The Lion Gods supply his headdress."

" He is Osiris the Lion God."

" I am the Lion God coming forth with a bow."

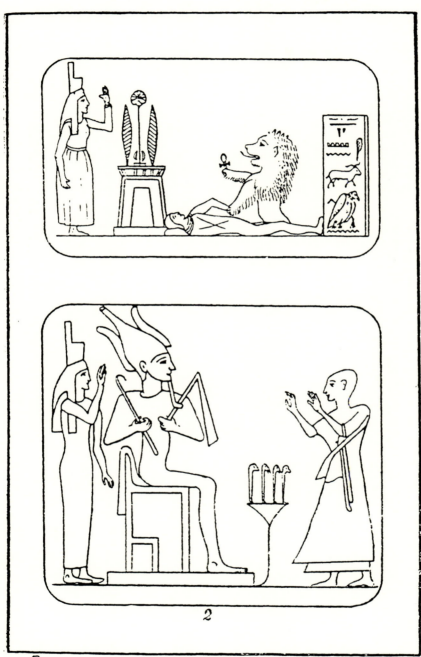

PLATE. V.

That the mysteries were magnificent spectacles there can be but little doubt, and that the doctrine was the highest that might safely be taught, may also be readily conjectured. The priests, clad in splendid robes, adorned with symbolical designs, received the candidate with all due form and ceremony; the prayer used at the commencement of the initiation is given to us by Apuleius, and contains the following eloquent words:—

"The powers of Heaven serve thee ;
"Hell is in thy command ;
"The universe turns in the hollow of thy hand :
"The ends of the earth are placed beneath thy feet ;
"The stars respond to thy voice ;
"The seasons return at thy order ;
"The elements obey thy bidding."

THE EGYPTIAN MYSTERIES.

The following account of the mysteries is compiled from Brown's "Stellar and Masonic Astronomy," Dr. Döllinger's "Jew and Gentile," and other sources:—

The Egyptian Mysteries of Osiris and Isis were in the form of a mystic drama representing the death, by violence, of Osiris the Sun God; the search for his body by Isis, the Moon, and its finding and being brought back to life again. In the celebration of these mysteries the Neophyte was made to perform all the mysterious wanderings of the Goddess, amid the most frightful scenes. He was guided by one of the initiated, who wore a mask representing a dog's head, in allusion to the bright star Sothis (Sirius), because of the rising of that star each year above the horizon just before daybreak, to give warning of the approaching inundations of the Nile. The word Sothis meaning barker or monitor.

The candidate was, by this guide, conducted through a dark and mysterious labyrinth. With much pain he struggled through involved paths, over horrid chasms, in darkness and terror. At length he arrived at a stream of water which he was directed to pass. Suddenly he was assaulted and arrested by three men, disguised in grotesque forms, who, taking a cup of water from the stream, forced the terrified candidate to drink from it. This was the water of forgetfulness, by drinking which, all his former crimes were to be forgotten, and his mind prepared to receive new instructions of virtue and truth.

The attack of Typhon, the spirit of darkness, typical of the evil powers of nature upon Osiris, who is slain, was also enacted, as the initiation progressed amid the most terrible scenes, during which the judgment of the dead was represented, and the punishments of the wicked exhibited as realities to the candidate.

The search for the body of Osiris, which was concealed in the mysterious chest or ark, followed. The mutilated remains were at last found and deposited in the tomb, amid loud cries of sorrow and despair. The candidate now beheld, amid effulgent dreams of light, the joyful mansions of the blest, and the resplendent plains of paradise.

Apuleius, speaking of his own initiation into the mysteries, says: "When all was concluded, I beheld the sun rising in full power at midnight."

MASONIC CLOTHING.

The clothing of the priests and those initiated are also matters of high interest to Freemasons. In the accompanying illustration (*Fig.* 2, *Plate* vi.), representing two priests in the act of adoration, the position of the hands at once and forcibly recalls an attitude not unknown to members of the Craft. Nor will the vigilant eye of the Mason overlook the clothing in which the priests are attired. The illustrations of Mason's aprons (*Fig.* 1, *Plate* vi.) are taken from plates, photographs, or original statues which are readily to be seen at the British Museum.

Wilkinson, in his excellent book, "Manners and Customs of the Ancient Egyptians," says : " The robes of the sovereign, when engaged as a high priest, much resembled those worn by the principal functionaries of the sacerdotal order, with the exception of the apron and the headdress, which were of peculiar form, and belonged exclusively to his rank as king. The apron was richly ornamented in front, with lions' heads and other devices, probably of coloured leather, and the border was frequently formed of a row of asps, the emblem of royalty."

That the teachings in the mysteries were veiled in allegory and illustrated by symbol is clearly evident. To have taught, openly, doctrines that are only fit for the highest developments of the mind, was an error such astute men as the Egyptian Kings and priests were not likely to fall into. To those who were ready to receive the priests were ready to give, but they did not put the food of strong men into the mouths of babes. All was done by regulation. Nowhere are the mysteries more happily referred to than in the "Sohar," a remarkable book connected with the visionary imaginings of the Kabbalah, written in 1300, A.D., in Spain, by " Moses de Leon," the English version being by Dr. Ginsburg.

" Like a beautiful woman concealed in the interior

of her palace, who, when her friend and beloved passes by, opens for a moment a secret window, and is seen by him alone, and then withdraws herself immediately and disappears for a long time. So the doctrine only shows itself to the chosen, and even to him not always in the same manner. At first she beckons to the passer-by with her hand, and it generally depends on his understanding of this delicate hint. Afterward she approaches him a little closer, lisps him a few words, but her form is still covered with a veil which his looks cannot penetrate. She then converses with him with her face covered by a thin veil. After being accustomed to her society, she at last shows herself face to face, and entrusts him with the innermost secrets of her heart."

LODGES OF INSTRUCTION.

Side by side with these speculative researches and their accompanying mysteries, by which the kings and the priesthood governed the people, architecture and the useful arts of life were taken by the rulers into their special care. They were dwellers in a land of peculiar advantages. The river valley, in which they built their magnificent cities, has no parallel elsewhere on the globe. Every year the munificent Nile, then as now, brought down with its annual floods a vast quantity of fertilising matter, and spread it across the broad, sandy plains as a thick carpet of manure. Thus enriched, the land brought forth abundant crops, with the employment of but the most moderate outlay of labour.

Still, man was called upon to do something more than thankfully receive the great benefits thus assured to him. The great flood of waters in their onward course to the sea constantly changed the surface of the land, dykes were levelled, old landmarks washed away, and, on the subsidence of the waters, it became a task of the utmost difficulty and frequently of despair to parcel out again to each man that particular piece of land which had previously belonged to him. Here, as we are told by Champollion-Figeac, the learning of the priests was extended to the aid of the sufferers. A few specially-selected men were admitted into the secrets of geometry, and entrusted with the teachings of trigonometry, so as to enable them to re-construct that which had been destroyed by the sweeping tide, with fairness and satisfaction to all.

From this we are well within the limits of probability to credit that other great secrets of art, more especially those of the builder, were entrusted to carefully-selected coteries. In these we may see the embryo of the Roman Colleges and the Mediæval Guilds, to which our attention will be shortly directed.

PYRAMID, OBELISK AND SPHYNX.

It is probable that many Masons may here expect some notice of the Pyramids, the Obelisks, and the Sphynx; these, however, present a subject at once too large and too vague to be attempted within the compass of the present work. The Sphynx, the body of a lion crowned with the head of a man, is clearly a symbol of the union of strength and wisdom; but its origin and history are alike lost in the dim mists of the ancient past. Mariette tells us that the Sphynx is older than even the great Pyramid itself. Of the Pyramids, so many and conflicting have been the accounts broadcast upon the world, and speculations concerning their origin and intent so wildly and so widely divergent thrust upon us, that it has become a hopelessly difficult task to comprehend either the lesson they may have been intended to teach, or the compass they were purposed to serve. A Mason will see in their triangular form an emblem with which he has special acquaintance, and he may readily discern beneath its name, which is Greek for fire (Pyre), the upward pointing triangular emblem of Siva, the fire deity of India. For those who desire to study further the meanings which are possibly hidden beneath the stone casings of the Pyramids, the ingenious theories of Piazzi Smyth and the peculiar speculations of Philo-Israel may prove of considerable interest.

With regard to the Obelisk, a book by Weisse (New York, 1880), written on the occasion of the transport of an obelisk from Alexandria to New York, contains some remarkable and extraordinary statements. The writer claims, on the authority of two gentlemen of undoubted integrity and of great eminence as Masonic brethren, that beneath the pedestal, whereon the Obelisk had stood for ages, were to be seen the insignia of a Masonic dedication. A trowel, a rough ashlar, a perfect ashlar marked with a Masonic device, and a pure white stone. A full conclusion on this unique testimony to the great antiquity of Freemasonry, an antiquity which we have seen the Rev. Mr. Milner, chaplain to H.R.H. the Duke of Edinburgh, claims to be " older than the oldest mysteries," can only be completely and satisfactorily appreciated by a careful study of the book itself.

The significant frequency with which Masonic symbols occur in Egypt gives indeed warrant for speculative research, and in no small degree justifies not a few of the startling assertions that sanguine admirers of the ancient Craft have set forth. In the language of

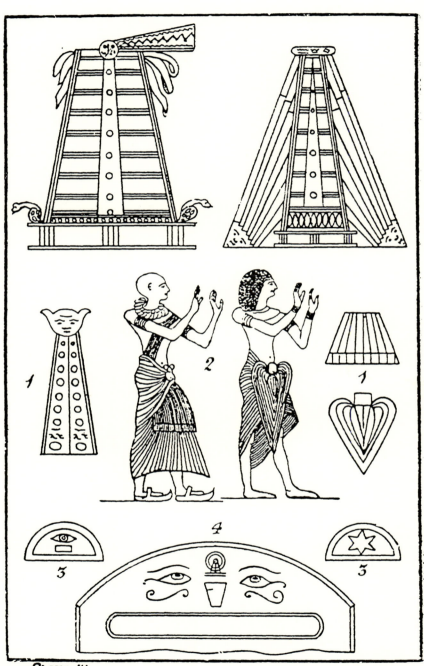

PLATE. VI.

the Hieroglyphics, a square and a perfect ashlar—is the sign employed to signify the word judge. A Mason's level, standing in like manner for the word adjust. Over the portals of the tombs of the Pharaohs may be seen the well-known Masonic devices in *Fig. 3, Plate* vi.

The illustration (*Fig. 4, Plate* vi.), taken from the tomb of Pentatour, who lived in Egypt in the days of Moses, gives so unmistakable a presentation of the Keystone that it may not unaptly terminate our present researches into Masonry into the land of the Pharaohs.

JUDEA.

BIBLICAL MASONRY.

As the Arab turns to Mecca, and the pilgrim hastens to Rome, so does the Freemason with instinctive sympathy bend his aspirations on Jerusalem. The ritual of the Craft, the language in which it is clothed, nay, the very names in which its teachings are personified, at once bring before his view the pages of Holy Writ, the land of the prophets, and the pomp and glory of the great Hebrew race. From whatever primal source it was obtained, it has undoubtedly been through the magnificence of King Solomon's temple that certain traditions connected with the great Masonic legend have been handed down to our modern lodges. It must, therefore, be an important part of our task to set forth, as far as possible, the progress of Masonry and its surroundings as they are to be found in the Bible and in contemporary history.

It is of little avail to seek much information from the Bible concerning Masonry before the days of Moses:

all we find there recorded concerning the days of antiquity is, at any rate for the greater part, recorded by the great law-giver himself, and is a terse, short outline, in which little beyond the quiet home life of a pastoral people may be discerned. We may point to the influence which the already magnificent architecture of Ur must have had upon the sons of Noah, upon Abraham, and upon those of his race who had lived in Chaldea before the great migration to Canaan. We may observe that the science of Astronomy, in which Babylon so greatly excelled, breathes forth in those exquisitely poetic words of Job, " Canst thou bind the sweet influence of the Pleiades or loose the bands of Orion ? " But, notwithstanding the building of the Ark and the construction of the Tower of Babel, we shall look in vain for a grip of the truths we seek, or a token of the hidden mysteries, till we come down to the days of the captivity and the Exodus.

To quote the words of so high an authority as Mux Müller—" Recent researches have helped to bring out the historical interest of the Old Testament in a manner never dreamed of by former theologians." Turning to the painted walls and to the hieroglyphics on the monuments and papyri of Egypt, we find incidents either closely assimilating to, or actually identical with the records of Holy Writ. In more than once instance the long famine, which is alluded to in Genesis, when Joseph warned Pharoah of the coming peril and saved his people from imminent starvation, is mentioned in the monumental writings. The following inscription, translated by Dr. Birch, of the British Museum, is taken from the tomb of Amen-Amenehma, at Benhiasson, and is considered by its age and other testimony, to refer, without doubt, to the seven years' famine spoken of in Genesis :—

"No little child have I injured, no widow have I oppressed, no fisherman have I hindered, no shepherd have I detained, no foreman of five have I taken from his gang out from the labour.

"There was no poverty in my days, no starvation in my time *when there were years of famine*.

Moreover, a papyrus now in the British Museum, and once in the possession of the very monarch who, during the nineteenth dynasty, oppressed and tortured Israel, has a history so curiously resembling the episode of Joseph and Potiphar's wife, both in the incident and in its result, that the following excerpt from its pages will be read with interest by all. The papyrus is entitled "The Tale of Two Brothers," and was translated from the original by M. le Page Renouf.

THE TALE OF TWO BROTHERS.

"There were two brothers, children of one mother and of one father. Anpu was the name of the elder, Bata that of the younger.

"Anpu had a house and a wife, and his younger brother was like a son unto him. He followed after his cattle, he did the ploughing, did the labour of the fields.

"Behold the younger brother was so good a labourer that there was not his equal in the whole land.

"But when the days had multiplied, after his younger brother was with the cattle according to his wont, he took them to the house every evening; he was laden with all the herbs of the field.

"The elder brother sat with his wife in the house and ate and drank whilst the younger brother was in the stable with the cattle. But when the day dawned he rose before his elder brother, took bread to the field and called the labourers to eat in the field.

"He followed after the cattle and they told him where the best grasses were. He understood all that they said and he took them to the place where was the best herbage which they wanted.

"And the cattle which was before him became exceedingly beautiful, and they multiplied exceedingly. And when the time for ploughing came his elder brother said to him 'Let us take our teams for ploughing, because the land has made its appearance. The time is excellent for ploughing it. So do thou come with the seed for we shall accomplish it.' The elder brother sent his junior saying ' Go and fetch us seed from the village.'

"And the younger brother found the wife of the elder sitting at her toilet. And he said to her 'Arise and give me seed that I may go back to the field, because my elder brother wishes me to return without delay.'

"And she said to him ' Go open the bin, and take thyself whatsoever thou wilt, my hair would fall by the way.'

"The youth entered into his stable, he took a large vessel, for he wished to take a great quantity of seed, and he loaded himself with grain and he went out with it.

"And she said to him—' How much have you on?' and he said to her—' Two measures of barley and three of wheat; in all five, which are on my arm.'

"And she spoke to him, saying—' How often have I observed the strength and beauty of thy youth.' Then she seized upon him and spoke evil to him.

"But the youth became like a panther with fury on account of the discourse which she had addressed to him. And she was exceedingly alarmed.

"And he spoke to her saying—'Verily I have looked upon thee in the light of a mother and thy husband in that of a father. Repeat not this again to me and I will not speak of it again to anyone. Verily I will not let anything of it come forth from my mouth to any man.'

"He took up his load and went out to the field. He came to his brother and they accomplished the task of their labour.

"Behold the wife of his elder brother was exceedingly alarmed at the discourse which she had held. Her husband returned home in the evening according to his daily wont. He came to his house and found his wife laying as if murdered by a ruffian.

"She did not pour water on his hands, according to her wont, she did not light the lamp before him, his house was in darkness.

"Her husband said to her—'What hath happened to thee?' and she said—'It is thy younger brother hath spoken evil to me, but I did not listen to him. I said to him am I not thy mother and thy elder brother is he not like a father to thee?—this is what I said to him, and if thou lettest him live I shall kill myself.'

"And the elder brother became like a panther. He made his dagger sharp and he took it in his hand. And the elder brother put himself behind the door of the stable to kill his younger brother on his return at evening to bring his cattle to the stable."

The papyrus then goes on to relate that through the information afforded him by his cattle who told him what lie in wait for him behind the stable door, the younger brother escaped, and after the lapse of some time the real truth of the case was disclosed to the elder brother and vengeance taken on the unfaithful wife, and, as a sequel to the story, after many extraordinary adventures, involving the wildest and most visionary necromancy, the son of the younger brother becomes King of Egypt.

Thus we begin to get those historic colourings which lend so important a factor in developing the character of the Hebrew race and preparing them for the rôle they were afterwards destined to play in the annals of the world. Egypt was the main land of their education, on the banks of the plentiful Nile were grafted the germs that later on in the low lands of Canaan appeared in the flowers and fruit of a nation whose history has reflected so important an influence on the present civilisation of the Christian world. It will thus be of the highest interest to seek out the formation of the character of these people, and see in what manner they obtained their knowledge of the great Masonic myth and through what channel they have handed it down to us.

MOSES, THE GREAT LAW-GIVER.

The great forefront, the colossal figure that stands out head and shoulders among those early surroundings—is the great master in Israel, the guide, the prophet, the law-giver, Moses himself.

The account of the infancy of Moses and of his afterward attaining a high position among his people and before the world, has a strong corroboration and parallel in history. Thus we read in Brugsch's "Egypt under the Pharaohs,"—"About a hundred years after the Exodus, a place is mentioned in middle Egypt as I-en-Moshé, which is equivalent to the Island or river bank of Moses." This certainly gives a strong reflection of authenticity to the received tradition. I-en-Moshé still existed, and was known by that name down to the time of the Romans, who, not knowing Moses, misunderstood its meaning and considered it to have in some manner relation to the Muses.

The extraordinary parallel case is that of Sargon I., one of the early Kings of Akkad, whose name in after years was adopted by Sargon, the great King of Assyria, an arched doorway from whose magnificent palace at Khorsobad has already served as a subject for illustrating the antiquity of the arch.

On an ancient pedestal found in Chaldea, supposed to have been that on which stood the statue of Sargon, is the following inscription. It has been translated by Mr. H. F. Talbot, who terms it "The legend of the infancy of Sargina, King of Algani," and thus comments on it—"One portion of the inscription much resembles the history of the infancy of Moses. We read in the second chapter of Exodus that the mother of Moses took for him an ark of bulrushes and daubed it with slime, and with pitch, and put the child therein, and she laid on it the flags of the river's brink."

As will be seen by the accompanying translation of the inscription, the similitude is in part identical almost to the very words.

" I am Sargina the great King, the King of Algani.

" My mother knew not my father : my family were rulers in the land.

" My city was the city of Otza-pirani, which is on the banks of the river Euphrates.

"My mother conceived me, in a secret place she brought me forth.

"She placed me in an ark of bulrushes: with bitumen my door she closed up.

"She threw me into the river which did not enter into the ark to me.

"The river carried me: to the dwelling of Akki, the water carrier, it brought me.

"Akki, the water-carrier, in his goodness of heart, lifted me up from the river.

"Akki, the water-carrier, brought me up as his own son.

"Akki, the water-carrier, placed me with a tribe of Forresters.

"Of this tribe Ishtar made me King.

"And for . . . . . years I reigned over them."

Accepting for a fact, as we are fully justified, the tradition of Moses being brought up in the House of Pharaoh as a Royal prince, endowed with all the great advantages and privileges of so exalted a position, we may be sure that the mysteries of Isis as taught to the chosen among the priesthood was a subject on which he had a full and perfect knowledge. The God of all time, the self-created, the soul behind the sun, the God of Israel, the pure, the perfect one, was the God he and those joined with him in the secrets of the inner mysteries alone worshipped. Egypt was in close communion with Babylon; we read of Tothmes II., King of Egypt, obtaining bitumen about 1400 B.C. from the pits of Hit, on the banks of the Euphrates, to aid in the construction of his palaces. Thus the account of the creation of the world, of the seventh day of rest, of the great deluge, of the building of the tower of Babel, of the confusion of tongues and dispersion of the people, which we now read in those marvellous clay tablets from Chaldea, so carefully treasured in the cases of the British Museum, were themes which Moses and the sacred colleges of Egypt must have had full and complete knowledge.

Nor was it alone in speculative theology and historical studies that Moses was occupied; we especially read "that he was learned in the learning of the Egyptians." He was the pupil and close companion of a priesthood who, while they themselves knew and grasped the great truths of the Eternal of Ages, saw the utter impossibility of entrusting such truths to the mass of mankind, the hewers of wood and the carriers of water. To keep these within the bounds of cleanly and decent life, to prevent a recurrence to the old time chaos of barbarism, arbitrary though necessary laws must be enacted, and men's minds brought to accept and obey, through wonder at what appeared to be supernatural power, through a mysterious and undefined dread of some surrounding evil from which the priesthood alone could shield them. Thus sprung up their magic and their conjuration; thus sprung forth the wonders which Moses wrought in the field of Zoan.

The imposing and stupendous architecture with which he was surrounded could doubtless but make an indelible impression on the mind of Moses. That marvel of marvels—the glorious temple of Karnak, with its walls of adamant and its magnificent avenues of gorgeous columns, was but just completed in his day. That he always bore the temple in view when thinking of a future resting place for the ark of the covenant is easily to be believed; that he handed down to his successors, and that King Solomon utilised certain important details of its construction in the building of the Temple, we shall presently have an opportunity of exhibiting.

Of the Exodus itself, and of the many ingenious theories of accounting for the passage of the Red Sea, we need make but little enquiry; but, during the forty years wandering from Succoth, to the Arnon, to Kadesh, and of the trials and temptations of the tribes through their many vicissitudes, our search into the history of Masonry will prove of fruitful avail, and we may close our inquiry into the wide influence impressed on the great Hebrew race in the land of the Pharaohs with the following fragment of an Egyptian romance, the graphic style of which reappears so closely imitated, in later years, in the beautiful lyrics of the Royal Hebrew poet. The Romance is called "The Tale of the Garden," and it belongs to the period of Rameses II., and must certainly have been well known to Moses.

"She led me by the hand, and we went into her garden to converse together.

"There she made me taste of excellent honey.

"The rushes of the garden were verdant, and all its bushes flourishing.

"There were currant trees and cherries redder than the ruby.

"The ripe peaches of the garden resembled bronze.

"And the groves had the lustre of the stone, nashem.

"The menni, unshelled like cocoa nuts, they brought us.

"Its shade was fresh and airy, and soft for the repose of love.

"When she met me, the daughter of the chief superintendent of the Orchards.

"Had sent her as a messenger of love.

"'Come to me,' she said, 'the garden to-day is in its glory, there is a terrace and a parlour.'"

THE TABERNACLE AND THE TEMPLE.

While yet the wanderings in the wilderness were but in their early days, Moses had ever in his view a habitation for the covenant of the Lord; the building of the Temple was ever prophetically before him. In Exodus xxv., we read—"And let them make a sanctuary, that I may dwell among them. According to all that I shew thee, after the pattern of the Tabernacle, and the pattern of all the instruments thereof, even so shall ye make it. And they shall make an ark of shittim wood." Here, light as the touch of a feather, faint as the breath of the morning, comes the first trace of Masonic tradition. The "shittim wood," of which the ark or chest of Moses is to be made, is the "acacia" of Freemasons. The "acacia" which marked the mortal remains of our great master, Hiram Abif. If proof were wanted, no greater testimony of Moses' deep insight into the learning of Egypt could be asked for than the detailed instructions he gave for the building of the Tabernacle. The master architect, the master Craftsman, in every branch, is plainly visible.

That these traditions were handed down with faithful accuracy is fully proved in Exodus xxxi.—"See, I have called by name Belzaleel, the son of Uri, the son of Hur, of the tribe of Judah; and I have filled him with the spirit of God, in wisdom, and in understanding, and in knowledge, and in all manner of workmanship. To devise cunning works, to work in gold and silver and in brass, and in cutting of stones to set them; and in carving of timber; to work in all manner of workmanship. And I, behold I have given with him Aholiab, the son of Ahisamach, of the tribe of Dan: and in the hearts of all that are wise-hearted I have put wisdom, that they may make all I have commanded thee."

On the death of Moses, his entrance into the Promised Land denied him, the building of a glorious temple to Jehovah, which was in the highest probability the great inner dream of his life, was unachieved and unattempted; but the great idea was deeply impressed into the hearts of Israel, and never departed from them. Joshua, with a vigour, a fury, and a fierceness unsurpassed in the annals of the world, drove the Canaanites into the sea, and led the tribes into the promised land. The "altar by the Jordan, a great altar to see," was sufficient indication that Joshua had in view the tradition left by Moses; but the great work was not destined to be achieved by him. The project was vividly present to David; but we read—"David would not build an house unto the name of the Lord his God, for the wars which were about him on every side." The great work was reserved to be the glory of King Solomon, under whom a temple was built, whose influence on the future architecture of the world can be proved to be far greater than has been generally suspected.

HISTORY OF THE CANAANITES.

Before proceeding to a consideration of the erection and design of King Solomon's Temple—an object of such central interest to Freemasons—it will be desirable to seek among surrounding and contemporary peoples, other than the Egyptians, for the various influences which they reflected on its construction. Foremost among these are necessarily the Canaanites, which remarkable people were still better known to the world by their Greek name—the Phœnicians.

The Semitic family is divided by Renan into two great branches, differing from each other in the form of their monotheistic belief, yet both, according to their historians, imbued with a firm faith in one God. The division as made by M. Renan is as follows :—

I.—The Nomad branch :—consisting of Arabs, Hebrews, and the neighbouring tribes of Palestine, commonly called the descendants of Terah.

II.—The Political branch :—including the nations of Phœnicia, Lyria, Mesopotamia, and Yemen.

Thus we see that the Phœnicians, or Canaanites, though sprung from the same stock as the Jews, were, in manner of life, more nearly allied to the Chaldeans and the Assyrians. Their earliest habitation was the shores of the Persian Gulf, where they were allied to the Chaldeo-Assyrians by the closest ties. About twenty centuries before the Christian Era they emigrated westward, crossed the Jordan, and took possession of the land lying between that river and the Mediterranean sea, wherein they speedily rose to a position of importance and renown in the world.

Their dealings with Egypt were continuous and intimate, and, overlying a substratum of beliefs and customs which was built on a foundation of Semitic and even of Tauranian origin, we find a thick layer of Egyptian theology, ritual, and observance. Possessing no originality of genius, they were, however, quick to adapt the inventions and contrivances of more gifted nations. Restless, eager, and adventurous, by nature both copyists and traders, they pushed their way for love of gain into the most distant lands, and were the first people of the world who utilised the sea as the great highway of commerce. Everything that could be bought and sold they traded in: like modern Birmingham and the Hindu idols, they provided their customers with gods according to any pattern they might choose to worship. They carried the beautiful jewelry and ornamental work of Egypt to the then known confines of the world, later on they dealt largely in the exquisite vases of Greece, and when these were above the pockets or beyond the appreciation of their clients, they made sham imitations of them, as boldly fraudulent in their way as the "wooden nutmegs" of Connecticut.

This peculiar physiognomy of the Canaanite is easily to be realised, the effigies on the sarchophagi in terracotta and in marble, which may be seen in the British Museum, in the Louvre, and in the Vatican, tell of a pertly joyous race, keenly alive to self-interest, bound by few ties, respecting none, laughing at all, finessing with craft and with the most delicate tact, and yet withal treacherous, bloody, cruel, and superstitious. No deity ever conceived in the whole history of mankind contained half the abominations of Astarte, their great goddess of love and vengeance. With one hand she granted all the allurements of love, and with the other she slew her victim in fierce and vindictive hate. The most odious customs of Babylon, wherein all women, from the highest to the lowest, suffered once during their lives an incredibly revolting degradation in the Temple of the fierce goddess, were carried to an excess by the Canaanites, that their more noble neighbours of Chaldea could never have stooped to.

Phallic worship, which saw in the principle of created life the immediate and active operation of the Creator, was pushed by them to its utmost verge. Not content with the abstract principle of Amon-Generator, the Vulture, and the Scarabei, as taught in Egyptian theology, they worshipped the tower and other grosser forms, symbolical of, or directly representing the underlying idea of their faith. To this worship we are indebted for those mysterious round and cone-pointed towers, dotted so plentifully over the East, and of which many specimens may be seen in Ireland to the present day. They are thus alluded to in the Bible—" And ye shall overthrow their altars and break their *pillars*."— Deut. xii. Brown in his excellent work, " Poseidon," says—" Another remarkable feature in Phœnician architecture is the use of the Round Tower Pillars, two of which appear to have been placed in front of the principal entrance of the temple.—Such were Jachin and Boaz."

We are thus in a measure enabled to estimate the wickedness of the people on whom Joshua poured out the vengeance of divine wrath, and it will be desirable for us to see what became of the remnant who escaped from the sword, and what their future influence upon their persecutors. From the sea ports, from Tyre and Sidon, they poured out in vast numbers, they colonized Sicily, Sardinia, the coasts of Gaul and Spain, while others of them, as there is every probability of belief, followed the western shores of the Italian peninsular, ascended the Tiber and the Arno, and founded the kingdom of Etruria.

ORIGIN OF THE ETRUSCANS.

Lami, the author of " Lezioni di Antichite Toscani," is a strong advocate of this view. He says:—" At a short period before the siege of Troy, the Canaanites or Phœnicians who had been driven out by Joshua, escaped from their seaports, and that some of them took refuge in Tuscany, making Fiesole their head-quarters." As collateral proof Lami goes on to point out the peculiar speech of the Tuscans, which, to this day, has a guttural accent and a remarkable use of the aspirate. Those who have lived in Florence cannot but have noticed this peculiarity of speech, so utterly different from anything heard elsewhere in Italy. Take such words for example as casa a house, and camera a room, these are pronounced by the Tuscans with distinct emphasis Hasa and Hamera, a pronunciation which cannot but recall the Sibboleth and Shibboleth which betrayed their brethren in the land of Judea, and which may be further exemplified in the Spanish words "don Juan" and "general" wherein the unwritten aspirate so strikingly appears.

Lami further refers to the peculiar similarity of the Etruscan and Phœnician characters used in writing, which as he says, unlike those of the Greek and Latin domiciled so early in Italy, are read from right to left like Hebrew and Arabic. As an illustration of this attention may be called to a comparison of the following specimens, one taken from an Etruscan Bronze called the "Chimera," which is to be seen in the Etruscan Museum in Florence, and the other from the Moabite Stone in the Louvre :—

(*from the Chimera*).   (*from the Moabite Stone*).

A comparison of the writing of the Moabite Stone with the Etruscan Alphabet, which may be seen on a vase in the Vatican collection, gives a still stronger confirmation of the similarity of the characters.

Taking the dates given by Ploetz, one of the best

German authorities on Universal History, we may place the conquest of Canaan at about 1250 B.C. Dr. Ginsburg, writing concerning the Moabite Stone, says:—" The age of the stone is about 900 B.C., and as no rational being can maintain that its characters were then invented for the first time for this public document, it is evident that they must have been used by the Moabite and other Semitic nations long before this period." The characters of the Moabite Stone are Phœnician, the Alphabet from which all the European Alphabets are derived. Silvester, in his "Alphabets of the World," divides written and printed characters into six main branches. I. Egyptian, II. Chinese, III. Hindu, IV. Babylonian, V. Phœnician, VI. New World. He gives the descent of the Etruscan characters as follows:—Root stock Phœnican, *second* Pelasgic, *third* Etruscan.

The Etruscans were a people given to many strange devices, notable among them were augury and divination, customs the Romans derived from them and carried to a very high pitch; also Phallic worship and its attendant symbols, curious specimens of which may be seen in the ruins of Pompeii to this day, were prominent among their observances. That such were the manners and the life of the Canaanites is clearly proved by the following quotation from Deuteronomy xviii. :—" Thou shall not learn to do after the abominations of these nations. There shall not be found among you any one that maketh his son or his daughter to pass through the fire, or that useth divination or an observer of times, or an enchanter or a witch, or a charmer, or a consulter with familiar spirits, or a wizard or a necromancer. For all these things are an abomination unto the Lord; and because of these abominations the Lord thy God doth drive them out from before thee." So strange and remarkable a similarity carries with it its own comment, and suggests an apparent conclusion.

Gori, the author of "Inscrizioni Toscani," is also of the same opinion, and points out many striking similarities between the Phœnician worship of Bacchus and the representations of the same cult prevailing throughout Tuscany, as pictured on ancient vases and tombs. Lami tells us that Nola of Campagna was educated at Tyrus, and that such a city existed in Tuscany down to comparatively modern times is proved by the fact that the Florentine Martyrologies states that Santa Christiana was martyred at Tiro, in Tuscany. Moreover, as further testimony, we read in Higgins' "Celtic Druids":—"Dionysius Halicarnassus states when Tarquinius Priscus had conquered the *Tyrrenhi*, or Etrusci, he received from them the ensigns of royalty such as had used to be borne by the Lydians and Persians."

Admitting, as seems fully justifiable, that the Etruscans and Canaanites were one and the same people, we have at once a means of accounting for certain peculiarities of architecture, the remains of which are still to be seen from the Tiber to the Arno. In the first place, those rude, though gigantic buildings, which are called Cyclopian, and which are composed of immense masses of rock, recall at once the customs of their ancient home. Layard, in "Nineveh and Babylon," exhibiting an analysis between the Nineveh remains and the temple and palaces of Solomon, says:—"First Senacherib sent (as Solomon did, I. Kings, v.), to the mountains to bring 'great stones, costly stones, hewed stones.' A terrace of hewn stone, at

Baalbec (possibly built by King Solomon himself), has a stone more than sixty feet long."

The peculiar style of sepulture adopted by the Phœnicians—on the side of a hill, hewn into the rock—such as we find afterwards in the sepulchre where the body of Christ was placed, was also in vogue in Etruria. This the illustrations (*Figs.* 1 and 2, *Plate* vii.) fully testify.

But the chiefest of the architectural devices that the Etruscans brought with them was the well guarded secret, the keystone of the Arch. Ruins of the perfect arch are found in abundance in all parts of Tuscany, but the most remarkable of all is the celebrated Cloaca Maxima built by the Etruscans for the Romans more than six hundred years before Christ. Pliny, who lived in the first century of the Christian era, speaks of it with admiration and expresses his surprise that it had endured for seven hundred years, unaffected by earthquakes, by the inundations of the Tiber, by the masses which had rolled into its channel, and by the weight of the ruins which had fallen over it. Since Pliny's day eighteen centuries have rolled away, and still the Cloaca Maxima remains as strong as the day it was built, still answering the same purpose for which it was originally intended. The arch of a Cloaca of possibly still greater antiquity, abutting on the banks of the Marta, is still to be seen in Tuscany, an illustration of which, taken from Denis' Cities of Etruria, is presented in (*Fig.* 3, *Plate* vii.)

One more suggestion is needed, and that is to note among the Etruscan remains, which from time to time are discovered, the number of palpable "imports" of Egyptian and Phœnician manufacture now to be seen in Museums, and which argue closely to the fact of an unbroken connection between the Colony and the parent land, and suggest, in the same manner as the name given to the ancient city on the shores of the lake at Bolsena, that Tyre was yet the mother of her children, and that communication was frequent between them.

We read in Mackenzie's "Royal Masonic Encyclopædia" that Tyre was one of the chief seats of the Dionysiac fraternity of builders, and that Hiram probably carried their rules to Jerusalem on his appointment there as principle conductor of the works. Of the special importance of Tyre as the communicating link of the Masonry of Egypt, Babylon and Judea, with that of Greece, Rome, Germany, and Great Britain, we shall refer to later on.

ISRAEL IN THE DAYS OF SOLOMON.

The days of wanderings were at an end; Judah and Israel dwelt safely, every man under his vine and under his fig tree. Solomon was firmly established on his throne, he had taken a daughter of the house of Pharaoh to wife, there were no enemies to rise up against him; peace and plenty, rest and abundance had replaced the ancient days of slavery, of homeless wandering, and of red-handed strife. The time was ripe for building the Temple of the Lord. The bitter persecution of the Canaanites was over and Israel lived on terms of amity with such of these people as had not been destroyed by the sword or thrust out homeless from the land. Tyre and Sidon were now in their highest prosperity, and had fully recovered from the effects of the terrible vengeance which the Bible narrative records. Moreover, the Jews having no longer the austerity of Moses to check and restrain them, and being possessed of the rest

PLATE. VII.

and advantage of a settled home, looked with less aversion on the religious rites and observances of their neighbours, and signs were already abundant that they would soon bow the knee to Baal and worship at the shrine of strange gods. Even David himself had foregone the old enmity, and unmindful that he, the chosen servant of the God of Israel, the jealous God, was in communion with an idolator of the grove, with one steeped in the abominations of Babylon, nourished a friendship for his neighbour king, Hiram of Tyre.

Thus, because of the friendship of Hiram and the relationship of Solomon's wife to Egypt, it is more than probable that communications between Jerusalem and these lands were not infrequent. It is, however, somewhat difficult to judge what may have been the terms on which Solomon stood with his great eastern neighbours of Mesopotamia, no word is given us at this period of any intercommunication with the two great cities beyond the Jordan. For many years before the Exodus the seat of government of the Chaldeans had been fixed in Babylon, 1675 B.C. During the reign of David, Tilgath-Pillser had built the City of Nineveh and founded the great Assyrian empire 1110 B.C. One small, though not unimportant link appears in a discovery of later years. The signet ring of Kurri-galzu—King of Babylon, 1300 B.C. (*Fig.* 8, *Plate* II.) is taken from Rawlinson's "Five great Monarchies," and is identical with the form which Freemasons have claimed by tradition to have been that of King Solomon. The coincidence may admit of further consideration when we remember that the Dionysiac fraternity of builders had their chief centre at Tyre, and that with them and their traditions Solomon had undoubtedly intimate communion.

From these builders and their connection with Babylon it is by no means improbable that the secret of the keystone of the arch might have been revealed. Every specimen of architecture known in those days was in vogue in Babylon. Diodorus says:—" Among other marvels of Babylon were a tunnel and a bridge. The tunnel was carried under the bed of the Euphrates, and was an arched passage, lined throughout with baked bricks, laid in bitumen, the lining having a thickness of twenty bricks. The width of the tunnel was fifteen feet and its height to the spring of the arch twelve feet. The length was about a thousand yards, or considerably more than half-a-mile."

Thus we see on every side Solomon was surrounded with nations well versed in the art of building, skilled in the practice of handling material, and having a deep insight into the mysteries of proportion and design. Notwithstanding the great teachings bequeathed by Moses to Belzaleel and Aholiab, Solomon knew well he could get no reliable assistance from his own people in designing and laying out plans for the building of the Temple. Willing hearts might heap up treasure to aid him and willing hands assist with rough unskilled labour, but for skilful design and cunning workmanship, even to the cutting down of trees and the hewing of timber, he must look for aid elsewhere.

THE TEMPLE OF SOLOMON.

With the wisdom, which was his special characteristic, he applied to Hiram, King of Tyre. The letter sent by Solomon to Hiram was, we are informed by Josephus, still extant in his day and kept among the archives of Tyre. But concerning the letter, the reply to it, and the subsequent building of the Temple, every necessary detail is so fully set forth in the pages of Holy writ that it would be difficult to add much to what has been written, and still more so to add anything that would be truly reliable.

That the Temple was not of vast dimensions is easily to be understood; its first object was to serve as an impregnable fortress, to which the precious Ark of the Covenant might be solely confided, secure alike from the danger of an external war and from the perils of internal dissension. (*See Appendix, Page* i.) For this purpose, "the great stones, the costly, the hewed stones," were needed. The Temple was at the summit of a hill, and the area of a sanctuary was greatly enlarged by building a wall up the side of the hill from the valley beneath, to look down which, Josephus tells us, was a dizzy task, and called for strong nerves and courage.

Josephus, dilating on the glories of the Temple, says the walls were all wainscoted with cedar, and so illustrated with works of gold that the dazzling splendour made everything about it look glorious. He further says that Solomon contrived a pair of winding stairs to be cut through the thickness of the wall for a passage to the upper part. A winding staircase, a device so well known to the ritual of Freemasonry, was evidently looked upon by the builders of those olden times as a work encompassing the highest skill. An inscription, called the bull inscription, from Sargon's palace, at Khorsobad, which was built but very shortly after the completion of King Solomon's temple, contains the following reference to such a stairway:—

"I had a winding staircase made like the one in the palace of Syria."

Another reference of the same nature made in the foundation tablets:—

"I made a spiral staircase in the interior of the doors."

Again on a tablet of silver:—

"With a spiral staircase, like those of Syria, I adorned its doors."

THE IDOLATRY OF THE JEWS.

Although both the Arab and the Hebrew peoples have from all time been strongly opposed to the construction of graven images, and although the tables of the decalogue expressly forbid the making of a likeness of anything which might savour of a graven image, "of the likeness of anything, in the heavens above or the earth beneath," even Moses himself flatly transgressed the letter of the command. In the tabernacle for the ark, constructed while the thunders of Mount Sinai still echoed round about him, while the vision of the glory of the Lord yet dimmed the blaze of the noontide sun, we find, as it is recorded in Exodus xxv., that the great lawgiver himself ordered graven images to adorn the very Holy of Holies. "And thou shalt make two cherubims of gold, of beaten work shalt thou make them, in the two ends of the mercy seat. And the Cherubims shall stretch forth their wings on high, covering the mercy seat with their wings, and their faces shall look one to another."

Layard, in "Nineveh and Babylon," describing the glories of Sargon's palace, says:—"In Khorsobad the winged human-headed bulls were on the side of the wall and their wings like those of the Cherubim touched one another in the midst of the house." We read concerning Solomon's Temple, I. Kings, vi., "And within the oracle he made two cherubims of olive tree, each ten cubits (fifteen feet) high. And he set the cherubims within the inner house, and they stretched forth the wings of the cherubims so that the wing of one touched the one wall and the wing of the other cherub touched the other wall, and their wings touched one another in the midst of the house. And he overlaid the cherubims with gold. And he carved all the walls of the house round about with carved figures of cherubims and palm trees and open flowers, within and without."

Nor was it in cherubims, in trees and in flowers alone that Solomon, in direct opposition to the commands of God, the God of Israel, carved graven images and broke the letter of the law. The sea of brass that was cunningly worked by Hiram was supported by twelve oxen. "The sea was set above them, and all their hinder parts were inward." And, moreover, on the plates and ledges of the two basses of brass, "he graved cherubims, lions, and palm trees according to the proportion of every one, and additions round about."

Mackenzie, in the Royal Masonic Encyclopædia, states that according to Jewish traditions the construction of the Temple was accompanied with a devotion on the part of King Solomon to the Phallic rites. That this would go far to account for the two brass pillars Jachin and Boaz which he ordered Hiram to make and place before the porch of the temple, may be readily understood. As we have already seen, such pillars were habitually placed before all Phœnician Temples; pillars such as elsewhere we read were to be cast down and destroyed by the express command of the Lord.—Deut. xii.

THE CONSTRUCTION OF THE TEMPLE.

In the sixth verse of the sixth chapter of the first Book of Kings we read :—" For without in the wall of the house he made narrowed rests round about, that the beams should not be fastened in the walls of the house." This was one of the Masonic traditions of the Jews, handed down from the days of Egypt from the mouth of the great lawgiver himself. Indeed, it was a special feature brought by Moses from the buildings of Egypt. We have seen that the Egyptians did not hold the arch in the highest favour; their idea of building was to construct temples, palaces, and tombs, that neither earthquakes nor the hand of time could destroy. They proposed, in fact, to raise structures that should stand as the monuments of their greatness to the end of time. The marvellous pyramids seem as though they were actually destined to carry out the aspirations of their founders, and the massive ruins of the Temple of Karnak, now some three thousand five hundred years old, bear testimony to the soundness of design and super-excellency of the work of those ancient Egyptian Masons.

In this very temple of Karnak we find the origin of the idea of the " narrowed rests " that Moses took note of and handed down as a legacy to the Craft. As will be seen in the illustration (*Fig.* 3, *Plate* VIII.), taken from a sketch of the ruins of Karnak, the beam was so placed that, while assured the fullest support, it was not possible that, by swelling, shrinking, or by superincumbent weight, it could in any way damage or weaken the great strength of the outer wall, having no force to thrust the walls outward, nor to affect the immobility of the supports. *Fig.* 2, *Plate* VIII., are also specimens

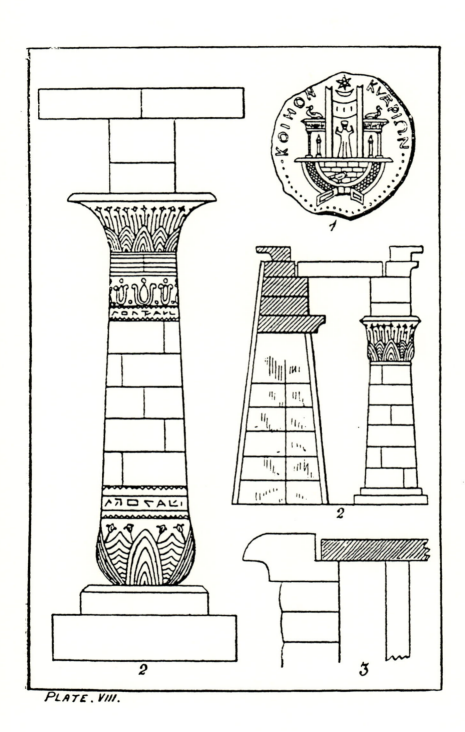

PLATE. VIII.

of the style and architecture with which Moses must have been familiar.

The account given by Josephus of the building of Solomon's Temple is very little worthy of attention; it is, indeed, but a condensed paraphrase of Scripture, and contains no tradition of value, such as might have been looked for in a work written by one conversant with the building of Herod's Temple, and who has been accredited with having stored up so much of the unwritten records of the people to whom he belonged. The only reliable accounts of the Temple are those in the first Book of Kings and the second Book of Chronicles, from which the following detailed account is gathered.

Solomon, having seated himself firmly on the throne, determined to carry out the great design of his forefathers in building a suitable temple for the custody of the Ark of Shittim wood wherein were contained the two tables of stone written on by the finger of the Lord, which Moses had brought down from Mount Horeb. Knowing that his own people were unskilled in the hewing of timber, he wrote to Hiram, King of Tyre, to assist him in his project. Hiram willingly agreed, and sent Solomon from Lebanon all the fir and cedar he needed. In the prosecution of these works not less than a hundred thousand hewers and carriers are said to have been employed. They brought down to Jerusalem the " great stones, costly stones, and hewed stones, to lay the foundations of the house," great stones which were squared and dressed by the builders of Solomon and Hiram.

Every stone and every timber being cut to its exact size and prepared to fit precisely into its destined place in the building, the work of construction was consequently pushed rapidly forward. The dimensions of the Temple are given in the Bible with what appears to be the most careful detail, and accepting the value of the Jewish cubit in English measurement at eighteen inches, as given in the ninth edition of the "Encyclopædia Britannica," and accepted by Fergusson and Layard, they may be quoted as follows:—The length of the Temple (I. Kings, vi.) is stated at sixty cubits, or ninety feet; the breadth twenty cubits, or thirty feet; and the height thirty cubits, or forty-five feet. In front of the Temple was a porch, the whole width of the building, and fifteen feet deep. In front of the porch were two pillars of brass, which, including their "chapiters," were thirty-four and a-half feet in height, having each a diameter of about six feet. The porch of the Temple, like the portal of the Egyptian tombs, fronted to the east, and the two pillars stood before it, that to the north being called Boaz, and that to the south Jachin. According to Wilkinson's "Manners and Customs of the Ancient Egyptians," Bo—is equivalent to motion, and Az—fire, from which etymology he considers Boaz to mean sun, and he states that the word Jachin signifies the moon, emblematic of Osiris and his wife Isis.

In the ninth edition of the "Encyclopædia Britannica" we read under the heading of "Temple"— "Another feature of Solomon's Temple is exactly reproduced on a coin representing a temple at Paphos. (*Fig.* 1, *Plate* VIII.) On each side of the door the coin shows a fantastic pillar standing free. Solomon erected two such pillars of bronze, eighteen cubits high (I. Kings, vii., 15), with capitals of 'lily work'—*i.e.*, adorned with lotus flowers like the Phœnician capital from Cyprus. . . . . Such two pillars, or twin stelæ, in stone, are of constant occurrence in Phœnician sacred art, and are still familiar to us as the columns of Hercules."

The inner part or great hall of the Temple, which was floored with fir and ceiled and wainscoted with cedar, carved in devices and flowers so that no stonework was visible, was forty cubits or sixty feet long. Within this hall were the brass lavers for the purifications, and the brass, wheeled basses to support them. There was also the molten sea of brass set over on the south side of the house, the great laver for the use of the priests standing on two rows of brazen oxen. Behind the great hall was the oracle, the Holy of Holies, where rested the Ark of the Covenant shadowed over by the wings of the cherubim.

Besides these were the courts for the priests, and the chambers against the wall of the house. The nethermost chamber, the middle chamber in the south side of the house approached by a winding staircase, and the third chamber. The dimensions of each of these chambers being exceedingly narrow and contracted. Prof. J. H. Middleton writes:—"In such small chambers the winding stair (I. Kings, vi., 8) can hardly have been more than a vertical post with footholds nailed to it."

The ornamental work of the Temple and in great probability the plan and designs, emanated from an inhabitant of Tyre named Hiram, sent to Solomon by Hiram, King of Tyre, who wrote concerning him:— "And now I have sent a cunning man, endued with understanding, of Hiram, my father's. The son of a woman of the daughters of Dan, and his father was a man of Tyre, skilful to work in gold, in silver, and in brass, in iron, in stone, and in timber, in purple, in blue, and in fine linen, and in crimson: also to grave any manner of graving, and to find out any device that shall be put to him."

According to Ploetz — "Epitome of Universal History"—we find that Hiram, King of Tyre, who had provided this architect and otherwise assisted at the building of the Temple, the date of which is given by the same authority as 993 B.C., left a descendant of the name of Phales, who was murdered by Ithabalus, High Priest of Astarte, in the year 917 B.C. This important occurrence may possibly be of use to us later on in our efforts to disentangle the knots of the tragic legend of our great master, Hiram Abif.

Although representing a building of vastly superior size (*Fig.* 1, *Plate* III.), giving a view of a doorway in the palace of Sargon at Khorsobad, which Fergusson in his " Handbook of Architecture " tells us was erected about 900 B.C., may serve to form some idea of the style of architecture in vogue in a neighbouring land and at an era nearly contemporaneous with the building of King Solomon's Temple. The winged cherubim, the pillars Jachin and Boaz, taken together with the significant fact that the architect and chief builder was a Tyrrennian, one who without doubt was in close companionship, if not indeed a leading member of the great Dionysiac fraternity of builders, all go far to sustain a conjecture that the style of the Temple was more closely allied to the architecture of Assyria than to that of Egypt. Thus we may safely conclude that the use of the keystone, so marked a feature in the Temple building of Freemasons, was also an actual and necessary fact in the Temple of King Solomon.

Indeed the art of building was fast approaching the period when the types from which modern architecture has sprung were brought into existence; the period when the domes, the vaults, the arcades, and the minarets that in later years graced such noble buildings as San Sofia, St. Peter's, Notre Dame in Paris, Westminster Abbey, and others, made their first appearance in the world and contributed so large a share to its beauty. In 586 B.C., Nebuchadnezzar dazzled all beholders with the magnificence of his temples and palaces. In the cuneiform inscriptions Nebuchadnezzar thus refers to a temple he had built :—

"With cement and brick I skilfully surrounded it; tall cedars for the portico I fitted, ikki and cedar with layers of copper on domes and arches and with bronze work.

"Its arcades close by I planned and with cement and brick its arcades I built."

The Babylonian also tells us how he restored the marvel of Borsippa—"the temple of the seven spheres of the sky and covered the pinnacles with copper."

In his book on Egypt and Babylon, Canon Rawlinson tells us :—"The royal quarter or palatial enclosure as arranged by Nebuchadnezzar seems to have extended some miles both in length and breadth. Outside this was the city proper, laid out on a regular plan in streets cutting each other at right angles like the streets of modern American cities. Ordinary houses were from three to four stories high."

According to Herodotus the construction of the city walls took 18,765,000,000 of the largest sized Babylonian bricks.

A "GRIP OR TOKEN" IN HOLY WRIT.

We have already noted, upon the authority of Mackenzie's "Royal Masonic Encyclopædia," and authorities in support of Mackenzie are not wanting, that previously to the building of King Solomon's Temple a Dionysiac Fraternity of Builders existed in Tyre. The very name of the society sharply suggests that something far higher than mere Operative Masonry was included within the tenets of the Fraternity. Masons who have not devoted much study to this subject will do well to obtain the valuable information to be found by a careful perusal of the pages of "The Great Dionysiac Myth," by R. Brown. Moreover we have most plausible proof in the pages of Scripture that societies of men known to each other by secret signs, bound together in a brotherhood, and called upon to assist one another in the day of trouble, actually did exist in the days of the Biblical narrative. Furthermore that this "brotherhood" was not confined to men of one creed or nation, but extended itself over a wide area and to dissimilar needs and circumstances.

This assertion is based on a passage in the First Book of Kings, chap. xx., 33, where we read:—"Now the men did diligently observe whether anything would come from him, *and did hastily catch it*, and they said, 'Thy brother Ben-hadad.'" A *résumé* of the history and circumstances that led up to this singular passage will bring before us its Masonic significance in a most startling manner.

On the death of Solomon and as a punishment of his idolatry the Kingdom of Israel was split into two parts. Rehoboam, the son of Solomon, became King of Judah, and Jereboam, whom Solomon had driven into Egypt, became King of Israel. The rival Kings of Israel and Judah were continually at war with each other. At a period of probably about twenty-five to thirty years after the death of Solomon, Baasha, King of Israel, sought to prevent all communication between the ten tribes of Israel and the two tribes of Judah, and built the city or fortress of Ramah as a blockade to enforce the intentions. Thereupon Asa, King of Judah, took all the treasure in the house of the Lord, that Shishak, King of Egypt, had not already despoiled him of, and sent it to Ben-hadad, the son of Tabrimon, King of Syria, who dwelt at Damascus, praying his assistance against Baasha, King of Israel. Ben-hadad acceded to Asa's request and Baasha was overthrown.

Sixty years had passed since the death of King Solomon. Asa had died and his son Jehoshaphat succeeded him as King of Judah. Ben-hadad, the son of Ben-hadad already spoken of, the grandson of Tabrimon, reigned as King over Syria, and Ahab the son of Ormi was King over Israel. Then came all those stirring events of which the prophet Elijah was the central figure. Ben-hadad, whose father had fought against Israel at the request of Asa, now entered on a war against Ahab, King of Israel, in which, in two campaigns, he and his army were utterly overthrown and annihilated, and Ben-hadad himself fell into the hands of his enemies. We have now clearly before us the exact relationship of Ahab and Ben-hadad. They were the sons of separate fathers, they were in no manner kindred, nor by any tie of affinity could they call each other brother. They were, above all, hereditary enemies.

We will now quote from the text of Scripture:—
"And Ben-hadad fled, and came into the city in an inner chamber. And his servants said unto him, ' Behold now, we have heard that the kings of the house of Israel

are merciful kings: let us, I pray thee, put sackcloth on our loins, and ropes upon our heads, and go out to the King of Israel: peradventure he will save thy life.' So they girded sackcloth on their loins, and put ropes on their heads, and came to the King of Israel, and said, 'Thy servant Ben-hadad saith, I pray thee let me live.' And he said, '*Is he yet alive? he is my brother.*' Now the men did diligently observe whether anything would come from him, and did hastily catch it: and they said, '*Thy brother Ben-hadad.*' Then he said, 'Go ye, bring him.' Then Ben-hadad came forth to him; and he caused him to come up into the chariot. And Ben-hadad said unto him, 'The cities which my father took from thy father I will restore; and thou shalt make streets for thee in Damascus, as my father made in Samaria.' Then said Ahab, 'I will send thee away with this covenant.' So he made a covenant with him, and sent him away."

Does not this vivid narrative carry its own comment? Ben-hadad has fallen into the hands of his enemies. His servants appeal to Ahab, the King, to save his life: and in Ahab's answer they diligently observe whether anything would come from him, "and they hastily catch it." What more natural than that Ben-hadad should cause his servants to deliver some secret token to Ahab which should cause him to return their salutation and to exclaim, "Is he yet alive? he is my brother." Then, as an act of brotherly love, which has ever burnt warmly in the true inner life of Masonry, he relieved his brother from the fear of death, "made a covenant with him, and sent him away."

If we may accept this explanation of the text, and it is difficult to see what other meaning can possibly attach itself to it, we have a clear certainty that a Fraternity, other than an operative guild, "a brotherhood of man," actually existed in times still in touch with the days of King Solomon. Moreover, we have before us one of the noblest examples of the practice of a truly Masonic virtue that may be found in the history of the world.

THE ESSENES.

In concluding our researches into the Masonic history of Judea, mention is undoubtedly called for concerning that peculiar sect, the Essenes, which preceded and in some respects anticipated certain of the Christian teachings. To couple their institutions with those of Freemasonry has not been unfrequently attempted, nor are there wanting certain grounds of resemblance to give colour to such a proceeding.

The Essenes aimed at living pure and simple lives. Affecting the extreme reverse of the principles of Phallic worship, they lived, for the greater part of them, lives of entire celibacy, neither holding women in good esteem nor admitting them to their secret councils. The lower grade were permitted to marry but the intention of the society was to discountenance "marriage and giving in marriage." They held community of property, led the simplest of lives, took no oaths, let their conversation be yea, yea, and nay, nay, and they were scrupulously strict in their observance of the Sabbath. They were, moreover, bound to assist each other in all their lawful undertakings. Amid the torn and confused rites of prevailing Judaism, tainted from its original purity by the idolatry of the surrounding nations, the Essenes held firm to their faith in the One God, the ruler of heaven and earth, and were entirely devoted to a belief in the immortality of the soul. Josephus, who does not, however, appear to have been a partaker of their secrets, nor to have been initiated into their mysteries, says they taught that— "To the souls of the good there is reserved a life beyond the ocean, and a country oppressed neither by rain, nor snow, nor heat, but refreshed by a gentle west wind blowing from the sea. But to the wicked a region of wintry darkness and of unceasing torment."

We thus find four important characteristics of Freemasonry—a belief in the Supreme Architect of the Universe, a brotherhood of mutual help and comfort, secret meetings shielded by signs and symbols, and a refusal to accept women into the membership of their conclave. Here, for the first time, we see women refused a share with man in the highest functions of life; in Egypt and in Greece the priestess sat side by side with the priest, and took solemn share in the celebration of the mysteries; but the Essenes, like the Freemasons, refused to accept their society. When contemplating the Monkish Freemasonry of the Middle Ages, we shall do well to retain the Essenes in memory, and call to mind how they gave the first impulse to a life of celibacy and took the first step to dethrone women from her high and proper sphere.

GREECE.

THE IMMORTALITY OF THE SOUL.

In tracing the Masonic history of the Jewish people it may have been observed that it was to the second or operative branch of Freemasonry that our attention was attracted. The higher branch, that which speculates on an abstract God and the reward of immortality, is neither treated of in symbol nor frequently alluded to in language. To the minds of Christian people it seems an utter impossibility to consider the great lessons for the instruction of mankind which the Bible gives in Noah, Abraham, Joseph and Moses, without at the same time entertaining the feeling that the doctrine of immortality and the hope of happiness in a future life were part of the instruction conveyed (*See Appendix, Page* i.). With the natural bias of opinion belonging to Christianity and to the age we live in it is not possible to imagine otherwise. There is, however, except in the exquisite beauties of Job, and the later traditions of the Talmud, but little on which to found our conviction. The Jew, as we read of him in the Bible, was governed by a mysterious God, who appeared in human form in the brightness of a dazzling light and traced with his "finger" characters on two tablets of stone, which Moses received directly from his "hand," and which were jealously guarded in a box of acacia wood, and finally treasured with reverence in a glorious Temple built specially to contain them.

No promises of reward in a future state are found in these tablets, nothing in any way to indicate the prospect of a higher and better existence in a life beyond the grave; man is directed to do good that his days may be long in the land, that he may enjoy the fruits of the earth; and he is deterred from evil by fear of the swift and pursuing anger of him who wrote:—"I the Lord thy God am a jealous God." Those high imaginings, those great strivings to discern the lesson taught in good and evil, in pain and pleasure, which so continually underlie both the symbol and liturgy of

Egypt, are never prominent in Judea, but we shall find them redundant in life and beauty as we consider the Masonry of Greece.

Before giving an outline of the Eleusinian mysteries from which so many of the rites of Freemasonry appear to be directly descended, we will record a few examples of the belief in the immortality of the soul as held by the great sages of Greece and as taught in the very arcana of the mysteries.

"The souls of pious men are amid the stars of heaven, and there, with hymns, celebrate the greatness of the Divinity."—*Eschylus.*

"Nothing is born, nothing dies, there is everywhere composition and decomposition, everything returns to that from which it came, and the depths of nature never change."—*Anaxagoras.*

"The prospect of immortality is a hope with which man charms his inner life."—*Socrates.*

"On us only does the Sun dispense his blessings, we only receive pleasure from his beams, we who are initiated and perform towards strangers and citizens all acts of piety and justice."—*Aristophanes.*

"Life only is to be had there; all other places are full of misery and evil."—*Sophocles.*

"Happy is the man who has been initiated into the greater mysteries and leads a life of piety and religion."—*Euripides.*

"The welfare of Greece is secured by the mysteries alone."—*Aristides.*

Concerning the teachings of the mysteries, we read in Cicero:—"Amidst all that is excellent or divine that your Athens has produced and diffused among men, there is nothing more excellent than the mysteries, which exalt us from a rude and savage state to true humanity. They initiate us into the true principles of life, for they teach us not only how to live pleasantly but to die with better hopes."

In the "Gorgias" Socrates says:—"Now I am persuaded of the truth of these things, and I consider how I shall present my soul whole and undefiled before the Judge in that day. Renouncing the honours at which the world aims, I desire only to know the truth, and to live as well as I can, and then when the time comes to die. And to the utmost of my power I exhort all other men to do the same."

How great the inner truths taught by these mysteries and the prophetic glimpses they caught of the great land of the unknowable, is thus clearly before us. Beneath the sheltering wing of Eleusis were gathered the great array of the sages and poets of Greece; men whose works stand as the type of nobility and grandeur for all time, in whose pages almost all the philosophy of our own day and the refinements of thought that soften and beautify life, even as we now accept them, may be found to have had their origin. Nor must it be supposed that the greatest of these, men like Æschylus, Sophocles, or Euripides, restrained their belief to the sensual fleshy gods of the Pantheon of Olympus, behind these jovial tricksters, behind Zeus, and Hera, and Aphrodite, behind the shadowy Poseidon himself, they saw the great Eternal in the heavens, the living principle, the lord of the length of time, he that sits and reigns paramount from everlasting to everlasting in the vast obscurity beyond knowledge.

Strespiades on one occasion wishing to vouch to Socrates for the truth of a statement, called upon

Jupiter to witness his words, whereupon Socrates sarcastically exclaimed: "Strespiades! Strespiades! at thy age dost thou still, too, believe in Jupiter Olympus?"

Like the Egyptians, from whom indeed the central germs of their belief emanated, the Greeks believed in a continual union of the body and the soul, they had not yet risen to that higher state of belief which is taught in the Nirvana of the Hindu, and in the doctrine that the soul is the animating principle of nature, a doctrine so happily put in the language of later theology:— "The body shall return to the earth from whence it came, and the soul go back to God that gave it." That Pythagoras, who obtained his doctrine of the transmigration of souls from the Brahmins of India, had an idea of a separate and independent existence, such as is taught in the theology of modern days, is sufficiently clear, but in the general belief of the Greeks soul and body were one, one alike in life and death. As the shade of the warrior passed over the fatal waters of the Styx, it was but the mere ghostly reduplicate of the body that had been burnt on the funeral pyre; grandeur of stature, nobility of mien, the stamp of the features, richness of arms and armour, nodding plumes and the wreaths of the victor alike entered into the dim portals of the realm of Pluto, and, in the well-known forms of the past, commenced a new career in the mysterious world of shadows.

In some ancient Greek statuary the soul of the dead is represented as a small child hovering over the body of the departed. This graceful idea has been carried on and utilized in Christian times. Among many instances may be quoted an ivory carving of early Byzantine date, which is to be seen in the museum of Munich, giving an illustration of the death of the Virgin, as told in the "Golden Legend." In this carving the figure of the Saviour appears behind the couch of the dying mother, carrying with him heavenward in his arms her newly-released soul in the shape of a little child clothed in spotless white.

THE ELEUSINIAN MYSTERIES.

Having now before us something of the nature of the men who received their teaching from the Eleusinian mysteries, and the abstract aim at which those mysteries were directed, we may with advantage turn our consideration to the origin and the nature of the mysteries themselves.

Both in Egypt and in Greece the greatest care was exercised to keep the mysteries a most profound secret. Clemens Alexandrinus tells us that—"the Egyptians did not reveal their mysteries indiscriminately nor expose the truths concerning their Gods to the profane, but to those and those only who were to succeed to the administration of the state, or to such of the priests as were most approved by their education, learning and quality." The jealous hedge with which the mysteries of Eleusis were fenced is constantly referred to by the classic authors, and indeed not only the legitimate custodians of the teachings, but the great body of the Greeks themselves, were alike anxious for the inviolate guardianship, the safe keeping of the mysteries. It is recorded that the populace, having taken up an idea that Æschylus had in some manner revealed or alluded to a matter concerning the mysteries in one of his dramas, they became so angry and excited at what they considered his blasphemous profanity that they were with difficulty restrained from tearing him to pieces.

Little, therefore, is to be expected from the pages of the older writers by which an adequate idea of the rites and ceremonies of Eleusis may be obtained. This, however, is in some measure compensated for by the accounts of later authors who, on the decline of the mysteries, ventured on descriptions which would have been impossible to their predecessors. Virgil, in the sixth book of the Æneid, is clearly if not openly their historian. Apuleius, transformed into an ass that he might see all the vices of human nature and brought into a state of happiness by the magic power of the rose, is another instance of the revelation of later days. There are, moreover, numerous illustrations of the incidents of the mysteries to be found in that great historical Treasury, the painted vases of ancient Greece. The illustration selected from these, which appears in *Plate* IX., is taken from Inghiramis' " Pitture di Vasi Etruschi," and gives a representation of the chief personages and objects around which the mysteries centre.

No lack of data is wanting to show that the mysteries were an early importation from Egypt, at least so far as the main incident and doctrine were concerned. They were, however, by no means taken bodily from the mystic representations on Lake Sais and the banks of the Nile. The Greeks, with their intense love for sensuous beauty and their delightful power of clothing the every-day facts of life with a poetic mythology, changed the tone and elevated the rites of Isis. The physical form of the dead body of Osiris becomes the natural course of the seasons, and the box in which the body was discovered becomes the Kalanthos, or basket, in which Demeter, the earth mother, presents man with the seeds of the golden grain and the abundant fruits of the earth.

The setting out of the story commences with the rape of Persephone. Amid terrible storms and thunder, Pluto caused the earth to open with a wide and frightful gap, into this gap he forced the beautiful maid, Persephone, and, taking her with him down into the lower regions, made her his bride and Queen of the realms of darkness. Meanwhile Demeter, the golden-haired, the mother of Persephone, with frantic grief sought her daughter through the world, importuning the Gods, especially Zeus, the father of Persephone, to aid her search. Guided by Hecate, the moon, Demeter discovered her daughter, and succeeded in delivering her from Hades: but, as the bride turned round and looked back on her departure, the Gods determined that in future she should spend two-thirds of the year with her mother on the earth and the remainder with her consort in the lower world.

Part of the myth, so closely connected with it indeed as to be little more than another version, is the charming story of Venus and Adonis. Adonis, Dionysius, and Phœbus Apollo, are, in fact, all names for one and the same object, the Sun, having to spend a portion of the year in the under world and the rest with those whom they loved or were beloved by on the earth. The youthful God, the young husband, the beloved one, is slain and lamented; he rises again, is adored, and panegyrised.

That this is clearly the old story of Osiris and Isis, the summer and the winter solstice, is evident and beyond comment. The direct application of the story to the Greek mysteries is as follows:—Demeter, in her search for her daughter, rested in the house of Celeus, at Eleusis, where, to divert her grief, she nursed

Demophoon, the infant son of Celeus, and her sorrow was lightened by the brilliant jests of Iambe. Having, by the command of Zeus, regained her daughter, Persephone, Demeter was made happy and caused the earth to bring forth fruits and flowers. She bestowed on Triptolemus an abundant gift of grain and a magic-winged car to convey him about over the fields and enable him to scatter the grain broadcast over the face of the earth. The sacred rights attendant on this she taught to Celeus, Triptolemus, and Eumolphus, and these became the founders of the Eleusinian mysteries.

As will be observed on reference to the illustration (*Plate* IX.) Triptolemus is seen seated on the winged car. In his left hand he holds the lotus-crowned sceptre and a sheaf of the precious grain that has been bestowed upon him. Behind him is the effigy of the Egyptian bird, Koucoupha, the symbol of divine beneficence. In his right hand he holds a chalice, into which Demeter pours a libation to Apollo, whose altar is on the right-hand corner of the plate. In front of the altar is Hecate, whose valuable aid had guided Demeter in the search for her daughter. Behind the winged car is Persephone, holding in her right hand the lotus-crowned sceptre, denoting her regal rank.

The altar of Apollo, which serves equally as a symbol for Dionysius and Osiris, must be of the greatest interest to Freemasons; it shows beyond all doubt that symbols identical in use and intention with those of modern Freemasonry were employed in the ancient mysteries of Greece. The disk of the sun, the double triangles, with the surrounding devices, each bears its own peculiar and unmistakable testimony. The altar and the myth of Apollo stood high in the estimation of

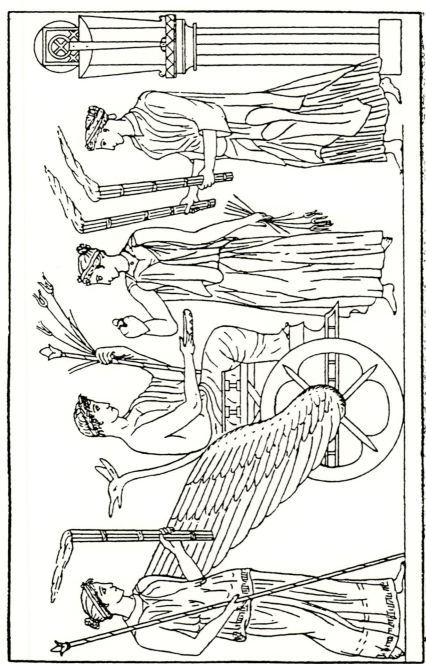

PLATE IX.

the Greeks. In their representations of the God, he sometimes appears on the veiled cone, or egg, an idea borrowed directly from the belief of Egypt; in the illustration (*Fig.* 3, *Plate* x., *Page* 82,) the segment of a circle surmounting the tripod is probably in reference to this idea. In some of the vases the segment is carried out in unmistakable egg form. In other instances Apollo appears leaning on the tripod, but always in an androgynous form, with the limbs, features, and tresses of a woman, holding the bow or arrow, or both of them, in his hands.

Christodorus describing the statues of the gymnasium of Zeuxippus, writes thus of Apollo—

> " Lord of the tripod stands Apollo there,
> Tied in a knot behind, his streaming hair ;
> Naked his form, so that to all who come
> Stripped of disguise, he tells their fated doom.
> Or that on all men the pure fount of day,
> Far darting Phœbus casts his piercing ray."

In other vase illustrations the figure of Eumolpus appears carrying a cornucopia, also an important symbol in Freemasonry. In several instances Demeter carries the basket already referred to or is accompanied by a chest, probably containing the seed which she presented to her followers. It is exceedingly likely that the chest of Osiris, the kalathos of Demeter, and the bag which is to be seen in the hands of the priests in the Assyrian sculptures, all emanate from the same main and central idea.

THE RITES OF ELEUSIS.

According to historical record, the Eleusinian mysteries were founded by Eumolpus, 1356 B.C., and the office of Hierophant was hereditary in his family for twelve centuries. The following were the officers engaged :—

   1.—Male and female Hierophants, who directed the initiations.

   2.—Male and female Torch Bearers.

   3.—A male Herald.

   4.—Male and female Altar Attendants.

The Hierophant at initiation appeared in a robe of regal splendour, and sat on a throne brilliant with gold, over it arched a rainbow, in the circle of which were seen the moon and seven stars. He was regarded as the representative of the Creator and bore suspended from his neck a golden disk, the symbol of absolute power and universal dominion.

Before him were twenty-four attendants clothed in white and wearing crowns of gold, while around him were seven huge flambeaux reflected by a number of burnished mirrors. His office was to instruct the neophytes after they had passed their various trials in the divine science.

The Torch Bearer represented the sun. His duty was to lead the procession of Torch Bearers when the wanderings of Demeter on Mount Etna were represented, and to receive the neophytes and prepare them for initiation. The sacred Herald imposed silence on the people and commanded the profane to withdraw.

The Priest officiated at the altar and bore the symbol of the moon. The Archon, or King, preserved order, offered prayers and sacrifices, compelled the victims or uninitiated to retire and adjudged all punishments.

The illustration of a disk of gold found in the course of Schlieman's excavations at Mycenæ (*Fig.* 1,

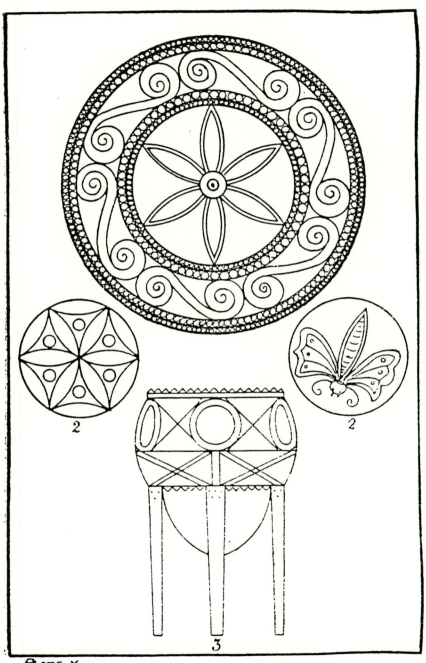

PLATE. X.

Plate x.) may in great probability be a disk worn by one of the Hierophants of Eleusis. The peculiar form of the interlaced triangles presented in the centre of of the disk was that in vogue in Greece, and afterwards in Masonic Lodges in Italy. They exhibit, as will be observed, the six points of intersection, from which an endless series of the exquisite designs so beloved by the Greek sculptors and frescoe painters may be produced.

The prayer to Ceres (Demeter) which Apuleius puts into the mouth of Psyche is an eloquent epitome of the mysteries :—" I beseech thee by thy fruit-bearing right hand, by the joyful ceremonies of the harvest, by the occult sacred cista, by the winged car, by thy ministrant dragons, the furrows of the Sicilian soil, the rapacious chariot, the detaining earth, the dark descending ceremonies of attending the marriage of Proserpine (Persephone), and the ascending rites which accompanied the luminous discovery of thy daughter, and by other arcana, which Eleusis, the Attic Sanctuary, conceals in profound silence."

The mysteries were divided into two parts, the one esoteric, the other exoteric, and these two parts were called the greater and lesser mysteries. The lesser mysteries, to which the multitude were admitted, comprehended symbolical representations of the history of Demeter (Ceres) and Persephone (Proserpine). The greater mysteries, which were taught to the elect alone, broke down the whole theory of the Olympian pantheon and were surrounded with the utmost secrecy as their promulgation in teaching the One God, "The Unknown God," would have given a mortal blow to the accepted religion of the state. It was said, when the crown of roses was given to the candidate in the greater mysteries, as a token that the course of initiation was concluded:—"Here ends all teaching, you are face to face with nature and nature's God."

The lesser mysteries were celebrated annually in February and March, and Strabo says that the Temple at Eleusis was large enough to contain from twenty to thirty thousand people. The participants were purified by the Hydranos, or water priest, a sow was sacrificed to Demeter (Ge-Meter, the earth mother) as a type of earth life and a grain destroyer, and the oath of secrecy was administered by the Mystagogue. The candidate was then told to "walk in the sight of justice, to adore the sole Master of the Universe; he is one, one by himself alone; all the others owe their existence to him, he works in them and through them." At the conclusion of the ceremonies of the lesser mysteries, the Neophyte was enrolled as one of the Mystics.

THE GREATER MYSTERIES.

The greater mysteries were also held annually, in the months of September and October, and lasted nine days. The celebrations took place in the following manner:—

First day.—The Mystics who were to be initiated into the greater mysteries met at the great Temple of Demeter called Eleusinian.

Second day.—March down to the sea, where all were purified by baptism.

Third day.—Sacrifices were offered to Demeter, the great earth mother, consisting chiefly of millet and barley. Having fasted during the day, the celebrants partook of a cake of sesame seeds and honey.

Fourth day.—The basket procession. This was the celebration of the Kalathos, Demeter's basket, which was looked upon as the protoplastic germ of all nature, it contained pomegranates and poppy seeds, and was followed by the chest in which were salt, wool, pomegranate seeds, ivy and small round cakes.

Fifth day.—The torch procession, symbolising the search of Demeter for her daughter Persephone, aided by Hecate.

Sixth day.—The sun dance. Dionysius Jakchus (Bacchus), torch in hand and crowned with myrtle, led a dance in honour of Demeter and Persephone. The dance having arrived at the Temple of Demeter, a square building, two hundred feet on each side, the Herald dismissed the general crowd, crying—" Hence! hence, ye profane ones!" The Mystics were admitted to the rites of the Photogogia (Leading to the Light) and the private or symbolic dances took place. They then witnessed a representation of the forcible abduction of Persephone, followed her across the Styx and beheld her wanderings amid demons and spectres and the terrible forms of the under world. Finally they were brought out to the light and saw the holy phantoms, awful but ravishing. On the wall of the Temple a mass of light was seen which transformed itself into a divine and supernatural visage of sweet but severe aspect. At the close the victorious God, Dionysius, who had brought Persephone through the dangers that beset her, was displayed as the Lord of the Spirit. The title of Epoptœ was then bestowed on the Mystics, and the participants were dismissed with a benediction and the parting words " Kogx ompax."

Seventh day.—Sacred games took place and the victors were rewarded with a measure of barley.

Eighth day.—Initiation into the lesser mysteries.

Ninth day.—The day of libation, when earthen vessels containing wine were offered as libations to the divinities of the under world.

From this it will be seen that many of the ceremonies had a striking resemblance to those of Freemasonry, and by the initiated a close analogy may be drawn.

It is possible that the schools of Pythagoras, in which practical science held so high a place, were in great measure similar to those held by the Egyptian priests for the purpose of teaching trigonometry and architecture. If it were possible to touch bottom amid the floods of folly and romance that surround the name of the first great tutor of geometry, he whose teachings gave birth in after years to the world-famous Euclid, we should find much that would still further tend to show that the Masonry of Greece, like that of Egypt and India, belonged to the first or speculative class, and taught without variation the unity of God and the hope of immortality.

ITALY.

THE ROMAN COLLEGES.

We have already seen that many centuries before the great city on the Tiber, before the fable of Romulus and Remus and their foster-mother, the wolf, was concocted, that the fairest part of Italy was under the domination of a race high in civilisation, renowned in architecture, and specially skilled in works of art. We have seen that in a probability almost beyond question they were in communion with their brothers in the city of Tyre, where the head-quarters of a great fraternity of builders had its chief seat. We have seen the mighty works the Etrurian builders did in the land of Italy, and above all the marvellous work they wrought for Tarquinus Priscus, the famous Cloaca Maxima, now fully twenty-five centuries old, still intact, still answering its original intention.

We are thus without doubt well within the bounds of fairness and probability in tracing communication of rites, mysteries, and speculative theology, of secrets and modes, of procedure in the operations of science and art from the Egyptians, the Hindus, the Chaldeans, the Jews, and the Phœnicians to the Etruscans, and from them to the Romans themselves.

The "collegia" of Rome have always been known to the student of history, but modern discoveries have placed them in a light which most closely assimilates them to the practice and identifies them with the symbolic emblems of Freemasonry. The illustrations (*Plate* xi., *Figs*. 1 and 2), are sketches of two exhibits in the "Hall of the Sarcophagus," room v., in the Museum of the Capitol at Rome.

Fig. 2 is the sepulchral cippus of T. Statilius Aper, measurer of public buildings. *Fig.* 1 is a Milliarium, marked vii., of the reign of Maxentius (commencement of the fourth century). On the back is a Greek inscription with the name of Anna Regilla, wife of Herodes Atticus, the stone having possibly served different uses at different periods. On the side which is of interest to Freemasons we may observe that the Roman "foot" rule was divided into sixteen parts. Its length is somewhat less than our twelve inches, being, according to the specimen under consideration, just 11·59 inches.

It is desirable to carefully note the shape and

position of the plummet and the square as represented in the illustration; we shall shortly meet them again in the furniture of a Masonic Lodge, where no possible ingenuity can dethrone them from their proper signification or sweep them away contemptuously into a "collection of tools in trade," as those inimical to Freemasonry have sought to denominate the objects on view in the Museum of the Capitol at Rome.

The great architectural works carried on in Rome by these Collegia, endowed with the traditions of their Etrurian instructors, remain to this day the glory and wonder of the world. Such magnificent structures as the arch of Septimus Severus, the arches of Titus and Constantine, the domed Pantheon, and those gigantic tiers of arcades which form the Coliseum, are glorious testimony of the perfection and excellency to which those Master Masons had brought their grand legacy— the keystone. The principle of the true arch was known to Egypt, to Chaldea, and to Assyria, as we have already seen, but the arches of Babylon and Khorsobad were only composed of brick, and are now for the most part but blurred mounds and shapeless masses of ruin, while the grand arches on the Foro Romano, built of almost imperishable stone and marble, still retain all the majesty of their original proportions, and, except where mutilated by the wanton hand of man, all their pristine freshness and beauty, and for ages yet to come will continue to bear glowing testimony to the value of the well-guarded teachings of Operative Masonry.

FOREIGN INFLUENCES OF THE ROMANS.

That the Romans thus provided with Masonic Institutions should propagate them in the foreign lands

PLATE. XI.

over which they held sway, is a matter that may well be expected and admitted. Of the vast building operations carried on by the Romans in our own land there yet remain abundant ruins to testify. At Cirencester, for example, are the remains of what at one time must have been extensive and magnificent baths, the tesselated pavement is of excellent workmanship and the coloured stones still retain the original brightness of their pristine tints. Beneath the baths are subterranean chambers called "the hypocaust," where are the furnaces and apparatus by which the baths were heated. The arches on the south side exhibit the use of the keystone in most definite form.

That the Roman operatives had recourse to native labour for their rougher work is certainly in every way probable, and our early forefathers had thus before them an excellent opportunity of learning the arts of the civilised world. Earle, in his admirable book, "The Philology of the English Tongue," says:—"The interesting question for us is—How far the British population was Romanised? Some think the habits of speaking Latin were almost universal, and they appeal to the rude-inscribed stones of the earlier centuries which are found in Wales, and which are in a Latin base enough to be attributed to illiterate stonemasons." Remembering the condition from which the early Britains were but so newly emerged, a condition, acording to Macaulay, certainly but little, if any, superior to that of the South Sea Islanders, and taking into account the falling state of learning, even in the highest places, during the opening years of the Christian era, we may readily forgive Mr. Earle his somewhat flippant sneer at "illiterate stonemasons," more especially as his "rude-inscribed stones" most evidently point to the labours of Aborigines who had had the grace and the opportunity to accept the teachings of the great Latin conquerors.

If the influence of the Roman Colleges be thus accepted, the reports of the magnificent buildings that were said to have been erected by our British ancestors in the post Roman period will have better foundation than hitherto to stand upon, and we may house Cymbeline, Lear, and King Arthur with all the regal magnificence our poets and chroniclers have claimed for them. As will be seen, when we consider the history of the Craft in the British Islands, traditions of Masonic fraternities, more or less reliable, are to be traced to a very early period in the annals of our country.

Down to the fifth century the history of the Colleges is still to be traced in the Eternal City. An imperial edict of that epoch was issued to the Grand Master of the Public Buildings in Rome to select for service from the colleges domiciled there, the most skilled operatives to carry out certain works that had been decided upon. In later years we shall again come upon their traces in the glorious structures of the Renaissance.

FREEMASONRY IN A.D. 79.

Our attention must now be turned to Pompeii, the beautiful Roman watering-place near Naples, which in those days was called Neapolis or New City. In the early years of Christianity, the exquisite little city of Pompeii, Roman by dominion, but Greek in its graceful buildings and in the culture of its people, was the home of a Masonic Lodge furnished with appliances and symbols for the teaching of Speculative Freemasonry almost identical with those now in use in the Lodges of England.

That terrible eruption of Mount Vesuvius, which in the year 79 A.D. buried the unhappy town beneath a thick carpet of lava and ashes, has hidden under its unbroken crust all through the long centuries down till the year 1874, a most carefully executed mosaic, now exhibited in the National Museum of Naples, and from which the accompanying illustration (*Plate* XII.) was copied. The following account of the mosaic is taken from " Rambles in Naples," by S. Russell Forbes.

" During the explorations in Pompeii in the year 1874, there was found a most beautiful piece of mosaic work which, from its wonderful and unique formation and workmanship, has caused much excitement. It is a mosaic table of square shape, and little more than a foot square, fixed in a strong wooden frame, and has been placed in the National Museum, Naples.

" It served as the top of the pedestal in the Masonic Lodge at Pompeii. The ground is of a grey green stone, in the middle of which is a human skull, made of white, grey, and black colours. In appearance the skull is quite natural, and the beauty of its execution is such as to render it a model of anatomical precision and truthfulness. The eyes, nostrils, teeth, ears, and coronal are all well executed. Above the skull is seen a level of coloured wood, the points being of brass ; and from the top point, by a white thread, is suspended a plumb-line. Below the skull is a wheel with six spokes, and on the upper rim of the wheel there is a butterfly with wings of a red colour, edged with yellow ; the eyes are of blue.

" The outline of the entire piece is symmetrical, so that the skull, wings, and wheel, through the protraction of the plumb-line, become halved. Looking sideways, the objects correspond with each other. On the left is an upright spear, the bottom of which is of iron, resting on the ground; from this there hangs, attached to a golden cord, a garment of scarlet, also a purple robe, to which some signification may be surmised; whilst the upper part of the spear is surrounded by a white braid of diamond pattern. To the right is a gnarled thorn stick, from which hangs a coarse, shaggy piece of cloth in yellow, grey and brown colours, which is tied with a ribbon; and above it is a leathern knapsack.

"Evidently this work of art, by its composition, is mystical and symbolical; at all events, it appears to have some reference to the Royal Craft, and as a proof of this last supposition it certainly has reference to some secret Craft in the old Roman era. The antiquity of the origin of the K.K. (Kings' Craft) and of the brotherhood, and its fellowship with ancient secrecy and mysteries, becomes at last certified by this wondrous piece of mosaic art, as acknowledged by affirmed known facts."

Whatever may be the value of the surmise thus made by Mr. Russell Forbes, one great, solid, unchangeable fact remains, the mosaic proves beyond all controversy that Speculative Masonry existed in the early years of the Christian era, and was illustrated by symbols identical with those in use in the Masonic Lodges of to-day.

The hall in which the mosaic was found is near to the remains of the Tragic Theatre, and but a short distance from the Temple of Isis, a much frequented quarter of the city in the days before its desolation, and centrally placed for the baths and houses of public amusement. On the adjacent walls are scratched representations of interlaced triangles and also small tablets with the emblems of Operative Masonry. Also in the house known as that of the tragic poet (Bulwer's Glaucus), which is not far from the Masonic Hall, there may be seen the double triangles scratched into the wall, in the form of the six points of intersection, as shown in the illustration of the gold disk discovered at Mycenæ (*Fig.* 1, *Plate* x., *Page* 82).

The hall itself is thus described by Mr. Russell Forbes:—" From the arrangement of this hall there is no doubt in our minds that here we have preserved an ancient lodge room. The number of the columns down two sides, the two columns in advance, the position of the pedestal upon which was found the mosaic now in the Naples Museum, the small room within the lodge, and scratchings upon the walls all go to confirm our belief. Note certain marks and scratches on the wall of the house in the street. A flight of steps lead from the hall into the garden."

A careful examination of the mosaic will be found to throw very much light on the accepted belief and teachings of Masonry at that most interesting period in the history of the world, when the immortal words spoken on the Mount of Olives were still warm with the breath of their inspired speaker. though they gave as yet but little spark of the great light that was before long to dawn on mankind and change the whole form and current of men's lives.

The first object which strikes the eye of a Mason on looking at the mosaic, is the square and plumb-line, the signification of which is so constantly and clearly explained in the Craft. The skull is, of course, employed as the emblem of mortality. The butterfly beneath the skull is the symbol which the Greeks always employed to designate the soul. The wheel is emblematic of the circle of life. The broad outer band represents the circle of the sun, and the spokes are so placed as to represent the six points of intersection, the interlaced triangles as shown in the seal of King Solomon, the central disk of the sun, the Purm of the Hindu-Brahmin, and the sun of the Royal Arch Jewel.

On the right hand side the rugged staff of the wanderer, the russett robe and the wallet of the pilgrim, clearly denote the passing, transitory life of the world. On the left hand the spear of the conqueror, the purple robe, the golden cord, and the victor's chaplet, exhibit plainly the designer's intention to show the reward of an upright and honourable life. The legend encrusted on the stone is without doubt an exhibition of life, death, and immortality, of the responsibility of the soul in its earthly life, and of the possibility of its achieving a life made glorious after its release from its tenement in the flesh.

The chaplet, which is to be seen around the spear on the left hand side of the mosaic, is of particular significance in Greek mythology. The vase paintings continually exhibit the chaplet as the ultimate prize of heroic deeds. On an Etruscan vase represented in Inghirami's "Pitture di Vasi Etruschi," Minerva is seen conducting Hercules to his seat among the Gods, giving him, as her last favour, a chaplet identically similar to that shown in the Pompeian mosaic.

The butterfly was in like manner used by the Greeks to designate the soul, and frequent instances of such custom may be quoted. The mosaic is of great interest in the fact that the species of butterfly accepted for the purpose is so clearly designated both in form

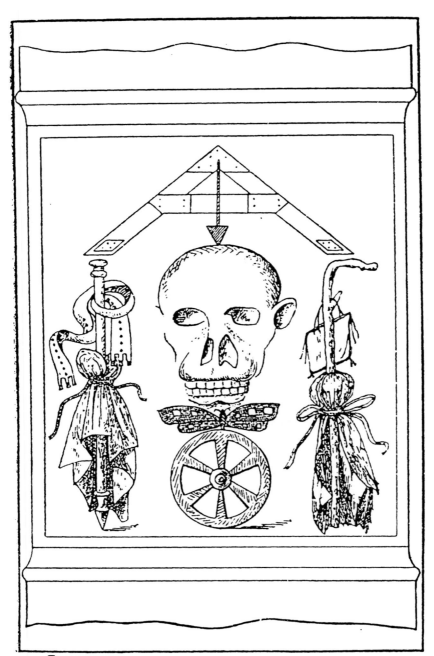

PLATE. XII.

and colour. In Gerard's exquisite painting of Psyche and Cupid at the Louvre, the butterfly is white, "the white, shining, geist" of poetic tradition, though this, judged through the testimony of the mosaic, would certainly appear to be in error. Nor was the idea of the figurative immortality of the butterfly confined to the Greeks and their era alone. Centuries later we read in Dante's Purgatorio:—

> ──── noi siam vermi,
> Nati a formar l'angelica farfalla.

which may be roughly translated as follows:—

> ──── we are but worms ;
> Born to form the angel butterflies of heaven.

As a connecting link in the history of Freemasonry, there can be no doubt that this unique mosaic, forming the pedestal of the ancient Masonic Lodge in Pompeii, is of inestimable value. With a single touch it proves that the Collegia and the Guilds were not merely a collection of trades unions or banded operatives, but that both Operative and Speculative Masonry were indissolubly joined.

Buried amid the silent ruins of the city, hidden beneath a desolation of lava and ashes for over eighteen centuries, the mosaic speaks of the ancient past with a surpassing eloquence. It brings before us a neutral ground upon which the dreamy Greek and the active Roman met in sympathetic harmony. At that period the builders of Rome, the Master Masons who hailed from the colleges of the Eternal City, were busily employed in Pompeii reconstructing the numerous edifices which had been thrown down or otherwise injured in the great earthquake of A.D. 63, sixteen years previously to the final overthrow of the city in the terrible eruption of Vesuvius, Aug. 23rd, A.D. 79.

During the period referred to, the colony of Greeks, who made the charming Pompeii their home, were held in the highest estimation by the surrounding Romans, who looked to their direction for guidance in all works of delicate taste and in the skilled intricacies of art.

Thus we had united the speculative and mystic teaching of Eleusis to the practical operatives with the square and plummet from the Colleges of Rome. How vital was the life of the Masonry thus unearthed from the ruins of the ancient city; how wide and unceasing its ramifications is told in the continuous record of the Masons of to-day.

Nor was it in Italy alone that Masonry spread its tenets during the epoch that witnessed the dawn of Christianity. The illustration (*Fig.* 3, *Plate* xi., *Page* 88), taken from notes on "Numidico-Punicque Inscriptions," by A. C. Judas, shows that Carthage and the civilisation dominated by that magnificent city had complete acquaintance with the symbols now in acceptance among us, and knew well the meaning which the symbols illustrated. The figure in *Plate* xi. is chosen from among six of the same nature; they are referred to by Judas as "The Tunisian Steles," and had clearly been employed as sepulchral memorials. The interlaced triangles, the disk of the sun, the crescent, the surface of the double cube, the "oblong square" of Masonry, are each so prominently displayed that their intentional significance may be readily admitted.

THE CHRISTIAN ERA.

Our account of the record of Masonry has now reached that period of the history of the world when the antique and modern meet and touch upon a common border ground. Egypt was no longer a leading light among the nations, the Gods of Greece and Rome had fallen from their high estate, and were regarded by the cultured classes either as fantastic idols or as the representatives of poetry and romance. The teachings of Pythagoras had expanded into the doctrines of Plato, all men were seeking something new on which reasoning beings could pin a rational fate, old landmarks were pulled up, old idols dethroned, but nothing new and tangible had been set up in their place. The mysteries were laughed at and their ministrations degraded into orgies of lust and excess. Then, like a star in the night, arose the teachings of Christ.

When we read these teachings in all their purity and simplicity, pictured, as we still can see them to-day, on the walls of the Roman Catacombs, it is easy to comprehend that the days of the mysteries were at an end. False Gods and delusive idols were no more needed, the whole truth had been revealed to every man, rich and poor, ignorant and learned alike. But the gross, benighted, superstitious world was as yet unable to receive the mighty truth, unveiled in its purity and in the absolute oneness of its entity.

Designing men sullied the immortal truths that had been taught, by their shameless forgeries and impostures. Heresies of every stamp blotted out the original simplicity of the text. On the one hand the words of the Divine Master were torn and twisted on the Scylla of the Arians, and on the other shattered on the Charybdis of the Gnostics. Arrogant and presumptuous self-seekers hid the light beneath a burden of miracle and mystery, and a lying garnishment of the supernatural confused and baffled those who sought for its pure and serene ray. Centuries upon centuries had to pass over the world before the great underlying truths could sweep away the furbishments of falsehood, of vanity, and egotistic ambition beneath which they had been hidden. Truly, the dark ages had arrived.

But amid all Masonry lived and serenely passed its teachings from generation to generation. In the early efforts of Christian art, in the illuminated missals of the monasteries, in the studios of the artists, in the designs of the great cathedrals, we trace its continuous career, and never fail to mark the symbols wherein its existence is recorded as a witness to coming generations.

CHRISTIAN-MASONIC SYMBOLS.

In Byzantium the Mason was early called upon to take his part in the pomp and magnificence with which the pristine simplicity of Christianity was to be overloaded and deformed. The great Temple of San Sofia was built expressly to outrival the great Temple of Jerusalem. Enshrined in gold and precious stones, enriched with all that was rare and costly the world could produce, blazing with glittering mosaics, lost in the immensity of its airy domes and pillared avenues of marble, one can well understand the joyous outburst of Justinian, who, at the completion of the work, cried aloud in his triumph—" Now, O Solomon, I have outrivalled thee in all thy glory."

One thing was remarkable in the Eastern Church, like as with the Hebrew and the Arab, idolatry was sternly discountenanced. Those marble poems of surpassing loveliness that the chisels of Phidias and

Praxiteles had given to the world were condemned to ruthless ruin, the likeness of man was banished on all hands and strictly forbidden to be reproduced. Then the ancient symbols of Masonry were called upon to represent that which hitherto had appeared in the sculptured stone or on the frescoed wall. The circle of the Sun again represented the unity and eternity of the Deity, the equilateral triangle again represented the Triune God, and under new significations handed down the traditions of the olden times.

But beneath all, the Greek converts still retained their old love for the poetic and the beautiful; the Alexandrine liturgy for the dead contains a pastoral as simple and touching as though it were a page torn from the book of Job itself:—"Guide them, O Lord, and assemble them into the plains of verdure, by the waters of repose, into the paradise of joy, where for ever are banished pain, grief, and sorrow."

Animated by such a spirit it is not surprising to find that the soul appears as a bird :—" That I might flee away and be at rest." Nor that the symbols of Pagan Greece soon adapt themselves to the expression of new ideas. The doves of Venus become the spirit of the Holy Ghost, the peacock of Juno becomes the emblem of the immortality of the soul. Later on, as the prejudice against the graven image melts with the flight of time, the Virgin Mother appears, homely of feature and mature in years, but dressed in all the glittering gauds and trinkets of a Byzantine Princess. A triple-peaked tiara surmounts her brow, rows of pearl, and collars of precious stones are wreathed around her, and a large golden ring, typifying the disk of the sun, encloses her head and bust. Still later, we shall find the Phidian Jupiter, a vast man of noble proportions, accepted as the likeness of the Eternal Father.

Nor was it alone in the monasteries of Asia, on the shores of the Bosphorus, or within the walls of Rome that the Masonic traditions still clung and lingered. King Solomon's temple and its symbolic teaching never escaped the attention of the Church. *Fig.* 1, *Plate* XIII., is an illustration of a miniature which appears in a paraphrase of the Evangels, dating from the ninth century, preserved among the manuscripts of the Imperial Library of Vienna.

The crux-ansata which surmounts the building is a symbol clearly handed down from the Masonry of Egypt, and the conical-capped towers, the round towers of Phœnicia and Ireland, the Boaz and Jachin of Solomon's Temple, convey their self-evident and intentional meaning to every Mason. As a curious coincidence, not without its internal significance of pre-conceived intention, is the beautiful Karlskirche, the most prominent sacred edifice in Vienna, built in 1723, presenting, as may be seen (*Fig.* 2, *Plate* XIII.), a striking resemblance to the effigy in the ninth century miniature, both in its cross-surmounted dome and the two historic pillars, Boaz and Jachin (*See Appendix, page* 2).

MASONRY IN THE MIDDLE AGES.

The monks of Rome early assimilated themselves to the building colleges, and, though edicts were frequently issued forbidding such unions, the needs of the monks as church builders made their union of paramount importance. During the time of Charlemagne, Masons were held in the very highest esteem. Later

PLATE. XIII

came the era of the crusades, when tumult and disorder raged on every hand, and it was only in the calm seclusion of the cloister that the arts and sciences maintained their life and were nourished. Let us for a moment glimpse into one of these secluded retreats of the Middle Ages, and see where, amid the surrounding gloom, both Speculative and Operative Masonry were nursed for the vast efforts they were so shortly to be called upon to undertake. Let us select the old cathedral as a type.

Barga is an ancient out-of-the-way city of Tuscany, endowed with the most incredible of legends, crowded with streets that run up and down hill in such picturesque confusion that the basements and garrets seem on terms of the craziest intimacy ; it is enriched with an inestimable wealth of artistic masterpieces and crowned on its central peak with an antique cathedral. So imposing and so sublime is the vast chain of encircling mountains, like the walls of a gigantic amphitheatre enclosing and guarding with jealousy the old-time city, that every pen would find it a work of love to dwell on their rugged crags—to paint their sombre rifts, green-clad or bathed in purple shadows, to point here to the softly-rounded hilltops, whence fancy hears the plaintive shepherd's pipe or there to the massive Carraras, jutting up like flames from the nether world and frozen at breath into fretted peaks of solid stone. He who, for the first time, could look upon such grandeur without bated breath or quickened pulse, has in him none of those sweet impulses that lift man beyond the brute, none of those fixed conclusions and vague longings that stamp on Man's mind the glory of his heritage in the beauties of creation, that whisper to and feed his yearnings for that sublime perfection to which, like a prelude, the loveliness of the world points out the way.

With mind thus prepared we are well fitted to enter the cathedral and study the lesson there presented. It is a building of noble height and excellent proportions. A marble wall—relic of the Temple veil—seven feet high and of solid proportion cuts the nave across On one side are the people—brutal, ignorant, and superstitious; on the other, separated by a hard and fast line, are the interpreters, the mediators, the professed priests, the professed recipients of revelation.

The wall is a cold and stony fact, it is no symbolic fiction, like the fanciful and delicately carved choir screens that may still be seen in many of the ancient churches of England; it is a physical robust construction against which the multitude may surge, and which but a slender defence would convert into the impenetrable barrier of a sanctuary. Behind it, the calm retreat of learning, the dawning perception of a road to lead out of the darkness and mists of the Middle Ages. and the first faint glimpses of the coming loveliness that was to flood the earth with beauty and the unspeakable sweetness of the new birth of art. Before it rude, unlettered men, boisterous in their lives, open to no convictions save those of the bludgeon and the sword, to be quelled only by their ignorant fears of the supernatural, to be wrought to better things only through the medium of their benighted superstitions.

Two epochs, two ages, stood opposing one another, one shrouded in the gloomy billows of blood and death, the other clad in the brilliant robes of the spirit of beauty and of life. It is not surprising then that with the ripeness of time we see spring out from the cloistered retreat into the very fore-front of renown a race of men half ecclesiastic, half laymen, whose talents had been reared and directed amid the incense of the altar and the solitude of the cell. Arnolfo di Cambia, Nicolai di Pisa, Giambologna, Dante, Cimabue, Giotto, the Gaddis, Fra Angelico, Michael Angelo, and a host of other great and glorious names who have stricken deeply the impress of their beautiful souls upon the history of the world. That most if not all of these were associates of Masonry the testimony contained in their works show ample proof.

THE FREEMASONS OF THE RENAISSANCE.

Let us first study the canvasses of the great artists for corroboration. We have seen how the portraits of the Virgin Mother were treated under the influence of the Byzantine fresco painters and mosaic layers, we shall now find a new conception has come across the minds of the artistic world. They have gone to Egypt, and from thence reproduced the goddess Isis nursing her infant son, Horus, statues and paintings of which abound in every Egyptian temple and tomb. The hard, ill-favoured type of the iconoclasts has been abandoned. Cimabue, and then his pupil Giotto, were the first who cut loose from the leading strings of the East and produced a young mother of natural traits and womanly appearance. One of the finest specimens of this period is the Madonna and child by Giotto in the old sacristy of Santa Croce, in Florence.

The Virgin Mother is seated on a throne, at her feet is the crescent moon, over her head are twelve stars, in her arms is the infant Saviour, on the breast of her crimson dress she wears, in gold emblazon, an effigy of the Sun in splendour (*Fig.* 2, *Plate* xiv.) On the upper right hand corner of the throne are two figures, one holding a Corinthian column, and the other a device strongly suggesting the crux-ansata and the lines of the altar to Apollo as used in the Eleusinian mysteries.

In the gallery of the Uffizi, wherein the paintings of the ancient masters are arranged in chronological order, are many pictures having symbolical marks of a similar nature. From these the following may be selected:—

On the right of the picture No. 27—" The Adoration of the Kings," by Pessellino, 1440 A.D.—we find the Virgin Mother seated, bearing the infant Jesus on her knees; in the centre is the ringed disk of the sun (*Fig.* 1, *Plate* XIV.), on the left hand is a dove, symbolical of the Holy Spirit. In the Egyptian Pantheon the Holy Spirit, Agathodœmon, is symbolised under the form of a serpent.

A picture of similar type, No. 26, by Lorenzo Monaco, presents the Virgin Mother and Child seated in the lower compartment, while above them is the device presented in *Fig.* 3, *Plate* XIV.

Here are indeed the Masonic emblems to embarrassment of choice and an unmistakable allusion to the Eleusinian mysteries in the ears of grain surrounding the life-giving sun.

The favourite subjects of the early renaissance painters were the Annunciation, the Nativity, the Crucifixion, and the Madonna. In a large number of instances the Crucifixion presents the Eternal Father as an elderly man of imposing appearance, seated on a bench, and having many of the attributes of the Phidian Jove; before him the Saviour is representing hanging upon the cross, and above the cross a dove typifying the Holy Spirit. A specimen of this class of picture may be seen among the exhibits of the National Gallery.

In the "Academia delle belle Arti," Florence, a diptyque of the thirteenth century, painted by Berlinghieri Bonaventura, has the crucifix of the "furca" shape, as represented in the Egyptian hieroglyphic symbols of revenge (*Fig.* 4, *Plate* IV., *page* 24).

A Descent from the Cross, by Fra Angelico, in the same gallery, has the following Masonic emblems (*Fig.* 4, *Plate* XIV.) prominently displayed. They are made up of three iron nails, an iron ring with spikes to represent the crown of thorns, and, in order that they shall in no possibility be overlooked, they are conspicuously laid out on a white cloth in a manner in no way called for by the exigencies of the picture, and can be considered in no other light than that of Masonic symbols purposely and intentionally displayed.

The attitude of certain of the statues which adorn the exterior of the Duomo of Florence is of such evident Masonic significance that the veriest tyro in Masonry would be struck with that which, by something more than a mere accident of coincidence, had attracted his attention.

The beautiful church of Santa Croce, also in Florence, is probably in its design almost unique among Christian edifices. It is a definite and clearly-marked Tau, identical with the Egyptian hieroglyphics for revenge, and the Tau of the ground plan of the great palace of Nebuchadnezzar.

THE MYSTERIES OF ROME.

Before quitting Italy, the great art treasure house of the world, we will for a moment return to Rome and take a short glance at the Sixtine Chapel in the

Vatican. It is a long barn-like room, bearing no particular attraction beyond the marble balcony of the choir and the inestimable frescoes with which Michael Angelo has adorned its walls.

Lent has nearly passed, Easter is at hand, the solemn offices of Holy week are drawing to a close, the walls are hung with black, no glaring candles illuminate the room, every circumstance which could excite the joy or cherish the hope of the beholder has been banished. Unaccompanied by any instrument of music, the choir sing the weird, unearthly strains of woe composed by Palestrina. On the epistle side of the sanctuary is a large candlestick upon whose summit a triangle is placed. On two sides of the triangle are fourteen yellow candles, and on the summit stands one white candle, isolated and alone. The office proceeds, one by one the yellow tapers are extinguished, a deep gloom, a thick darkness, appears to settle down upon the chapel. The singers continue their mournful chaunt, earth seems fading away and passing from the grasp, the night of darkness is at hand. Wings of terror flap in the dim vault above, and spirits of evil strive to thrust back the piercing despair of the choir, the low muttered supplications of the altar. But one light, the white taper on the apex of the triangle, remains; shortly that is removed and hidden behind the hangings of the altar. Gloom, terror, and despair are on every hand. But with the dawn of Easter the lights return to the temple, the trumpets blast forth their brazen notes of joy, and a thousand throats resound, Hosanna ! Hosanna ! Christ is risen from the dead.

The mysteries of Rome have again been presented to the people, the Sun has passed the vernal equinox

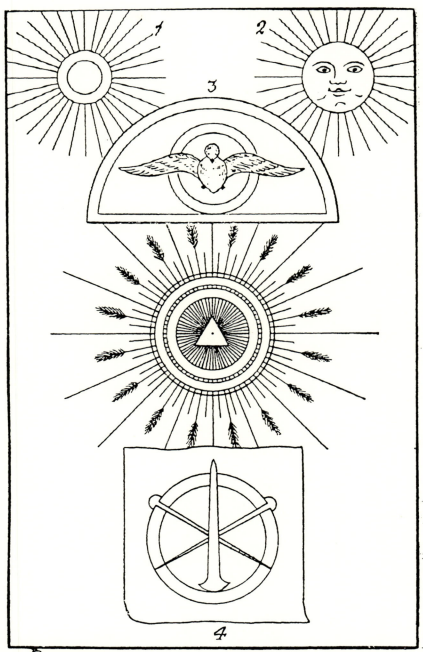

PLATE. XIV.

and mounts triumphantly on his path to the summer solstice, again to bless the earth with joy and splendour.

GERMANY.

THE SCANDINAVIAN LEGEND.

The annals of Germany are rich in Masonic history and tradition, but before taking them into consideration it will be advantageous to trace the mystic records which the northern kinsmen of the Germans have to exhibit in their celebrated Scandinavian Legends. The particular legend which is interesting to Freemasons is that of the death and regeneration of Baldur, son of Odin, bearing as it does so strong a central resemblance to the legends of Osiris and Isis, of Demeter and Persephone, and to that of the death of our Grand Master, Hiram Abif.

The legend is collected from the pages of Thorpe's "Northern Mythology," and is here presented in condensed and connected form.

Odin, the "all father," creator of gods and men in the ancient world of the North, had a son, Baldur, brighter than the brightness of the morning. So fair was he of aspect, and so bright, that the very light of day issued from his countenance. Wise and eloquent was he, and so gifted that none might pervert his judgment. He abode in the serenity of heaven, in the place called Breidbakh, so pure and exalted that nothing evil can enter there.

But ill-dreams troubled the heart of Baldur. Ever as night came, and sleep lay with him on his couch, fear and trembling seized upon him; his being was threatened in his dreams, he went nightly in danger of his life.

Then Friga, his mother—Friga the great, the noble one—called together the gods of the air, the gods of the earth and the water, from them she exacted an oath; an oath she took from the gods of fire and of iron, from the gods of all metals, of stone, of earth, of trees, of diseases, of all beasts, and bears, and venomous snakes that they would not hurt her son.

To drive the evil omens from his mind, Friga charged her son to stand forth in the great assembly and let all the world shoot at him with bows, to let them strike at him with mighty clubs, or hurl on him the ponderous rock. The ordeal was passed, neither arrow, nor hammer, nor rock could harm him. He passed through the shafts of the world unscathed, unharmed.

Still the terrors of the night were ever with him; the poison of his dreams wrought a fever in his blood, and he could find no rest.

Thereupon Odin, who loved his son with a surpassing love, determined to put an end to suspense. He bent his will to the task. He called forth his bright steed and resolved to ride to the dread regions of the world beneath. He strode forth on the way. He took the road to Nifel by the eastern gate of Hel. There lay the grave of the dead Vala. By the dreadness of his might he would call her back to life and draw from her the future of his beloved Baldur.

The fierce dog of Hel, with bloody breast and jaws, bayed and howled at him, and sought to render him to pieces. But Odin heeded him not—he rode straight on to the Vala's grave. There he uttered with bated breath the fearful words that awake and raise the dead. Vala comes forth; she bursts the cruel bondage of the tomb. In a few and mystic words she tells the manner of Odin's death; but neither detail nor circumstance will she tell, nor in what manner it may be avoided.

Odin, stung by her refusal, treats her with scorn, insultingly exclaims: "No Vala art thou: thou knowest not the hidden secrets of the coming day, neither Vala nor wise woman art thou." Thereon the Vala with anger, with fearful hate replies: "Ride home and make thy boast: Thou hast called the Vala from the chill repose of the grave, but never again shall mortal behold me till Loki shall have burst his chains and Ragnaröck be come."

Loki, envious in his heart—he who loved not Baldur because of his brightness and his glory—disguised himself as a woman, and, hidden in the garb of a maiden, took himself to the shooting, where all with unabated might still sought, though sought in vain, to wound the bright, the noble one—Baldur, the son of Odin.

To Odin's mother, Friga, Loki betook himself, and sought with cunning words to learn the secret charm which defied the club, the spear, the arrow. Then Friga told him no fire, no water, nor iron could hurt her son, neither earth, nor stone, nor trees, nor beasts, nor bears, nor venomed snakes. None of these could avail in aught against him.

Then Loki, he the secret, cunning one, took from the tree a spray of mistletoe, green in the leaf and budding into bloom. To Höd, blind and unarmed, he bore it, telling him with that to shoot the unassailable.

Höd shot with the tender spray. It pierced Baldur to the heart. He fell pierced through, to the earth he fell; Baldur was dead.

Bitter was the moaning, loud the lamentations, shrill were the cries of grief, they took up his corpse. They placed his corpse upon a bier. Down to the sea, to the shore of the great sea they bore it, by the waves of the raging sea they stood it down. With labour and much toil they got afloat the great ship whereon his body was to be burned.

His wife, Nanna, the lovely one, grieved for him with such fierce and bitter grief that the bonds of her heart burst; they burst, they snapt in sunder, and Nanna was laid on the funeral pile beside her beloved Baldur. His horse, too, the swift companion of his days, he, too, was thrown upon the pile, and they floated on the sea, the great, the encircling sea.

Then the fire ascended, the smoke rose up to heaven, and the sorrowing earth was bereft of the bright, the good, the noble Baldur, the fair, the shining son of Odin.

Swiftly to Hel rode Hermod, Hermod the brother of Baldur, rode to recall him back to earth. There he beheld him, his brother the shining one, seated on the highest throne, seated on the throne of honour. To Hel, he clamoured, he recounted the grief of all the world at the loss of one so noble and so good. Hel heard his words, he listened to Hermod as with eloquence he pleaded that Baldur might return. "Go," said the dim arbiter of the land of ghosts and shadows, " go back to earth, and if in perfect truth the whole world weeps for Baldur, then shall he return again to bless them.

He went, with haste he flew, his steed with impatient strides tore through the bounds of space. The whole world wept—all men, all beasts, all birds, all wood, all stone, all metals wept. One eye alone was dry.

Thökt, an ancient giantess, a sorceress, a hideous crone, she who lived in a desert cavern on a mountain side, neither tear nor moan gave she. Hermod came to her, he demanded of her "Why weep ye not, why sorrow ye not for the return of Baldur." With scornful laugh she answered him, she replied:—

"Yes, Thökt will wail, weep with dry tears for Baldur's death; breathes he or dies he, it boots me not; let him bide with Hel."

Then came the truth to light. Vali, Odin's infant, new-born son, slew Höd. All men knew that Thökt was Loki, who had brought about the death of Baldur, and prevented his release from Hel. They rose up against him, they swore a speedy vengeance, they swore by the bounds of the encircling sea that Baldur should be avenged, that Loki should not escape them.

So Loki—he, the envious one, the secret, cunning one—changed himself again, changed into the likeness of a salmon, and jumped into the stream. But they, the Æsir, saw him; they knew his cunning, they knew his cunning and his tricks. They made a net, a strong net, of hemp they made it, they threw it into the waterfall; they cast it where they saw the bright shining of his scales. But Loki hid between two stones, and the net passed over him.

Again they threw the net. They tied things heavy to the meshes of the net so that nothing could slip away from beneath it. But Loki flew before them, till, pressed by the rushing of the water, he feared to be pushed into the open sea, the great, the fearful sea. Then, he turned round upon his pursuers, leapt over the net, and returned to the shelter of the waterfall.

Swiftly they came back to the rocks, Thor wading in the middle of the stream. Now must Loki fly past his enemies and risk his life to the terrors of the sea or again leap the waterfall. He leaps—he sought to leap, but Thor caught him by the tail. They have him, in their hands they hold him; his enemies have triumphed.

They take him, the avenging gods take him. They bind him fast, with bands of iron they bind him, deep in the earth they buried him. There will he lay fast bound and firm until the end shall come, until the day of Ragnärock.

Then shall fall the thickest horrors of the winter. One wolf will swallow up the sun, another wolf will swallow up the moon; Midgard's serpent will blow forth her venom; the dog of Garm shall be loosed, Thor will slay the serpent, but will die from the venom of his breath. The wolf will slay Odin, but Vali will come forth and slay the wolf. The Surt will hurl fire all over the earth, and heaven and earth shall be no more.

After this, a new earth will arise a second time from the ocean, plentiful and verdant in its beauty. The Æsir shall meet again on Ida's plains. Unsown fields shall bear fruit, all evils shall cease. Baldur shall return and dwell in Odin's noble hall. In Gimli, the clear heaven of delight, there will be a hall brighter than the sun, roofed in with gold, and there virtuous people shall dwell in happiness for ever.

Even Loki shall burst his bonds and Ragnärock, the twiligt of the gods, shall have come. Then shall the Mighthy One from above enter the council of the gods and establish a reign of peace that shall remain unbroken for ever.

Again, we have the story of the dying Sun and his revival after a period of deprivation and sorrow. Again, we see the bright and beautiful Persephone torn from the arms of her mother to the mysteries of Hades, and again returned that the earth might be blessed with plenty, Baldur is slain; he journeys to Hel. Höd, the spirit of darkness, has slain him. His mother, the fruitful earth, mourns for him, all nature is filled with weeping; darkness prevails, the earth stiffens, but Vali burst its frozen rind, and the clear days of life come back again.

THE ERA OF CHARLEMAGNE.

With the decadence of the Roman Empire and the subsidence of the frantic energy displayed by the northern barbarians in their fiery career of conquest, of destruction and plunder, an era of general apathy, indeed of general stupidity, seems to have occupied the world. The arts and sciences banished from their thrones hid in unknown solitudes and timidly withdrew from the congregations of men. Beneath an ever present oppression, sometimes appalling in its bloodthirsty fierceness, sometimes apathetic in its cynical toleration, the Christians of Rome emerged from the cloud in which ignorance and brutality had sought to conceal them. With their advent into life came the Basilica, a simple adaptation of existing edifices to the needs of their system of worship. The front porch, the circular arch, the column-bordered nave, the main altar, and the tribune composed the principal features of their temples. Spreading eastward from Rome, Christian art rapidly developed itself, as we have already seen, into new forms and more ambitious designs. But in the west the progress was slow. After the might of Rome had sunk, the form of her great Prefectures still continued for some time to remain under the same geographical expressions the great mistress of the world had left them. But they gradually sunk into a lethargic trance, wherein the new arts of civilisation they had learned from their conquerors and the fierce activity of their days of barbarism alike had left them, a prey to despair, to inanition and to ruin.

Soon after this the new creed of Islamism was established, and its upholders pushed a career of conquest unparalleled in the history of the world. India, Persia, Syria, Palestine, Egypt, Tunis, Morocco, and Spain had fallen before the might of their arms, and it seemed as though in their prowess they would over-run and dominate the whole of the continent of Europe. Their renowned general, Abdéraman, has reduced to ashes all the country from the Garonne to the Loire, and was about to invade the rich sanctuary of St. Martin, at Tours. There, however, he was killed, and his forces utterly routed in a furious battle by Charles Martel (Charles, the Hammer of God), three hundred thousand of his followers slain and the menace of Europe shattered to pieces.

A peace from outer enemies being thus established, Charlemagne, in his day, was enabled to consolidate a magnificent empire from the Elbe to the Pyrenees, from the Mediterranean to the North Sea. His alliance with the Pope spread the orthodox faith of the Roman Church far and wide through Europe, and on every side Churches and religious houses for the propagation of Christianity were erected. Previously to the ninth century the houses were mostly constructed of wood, but Charlemagne brought in an era of stone. Every encouragement in his power he gave to the Masons he brought with him from Rome, some of whom were clerics, some laymen, and all were possessed of the legends which had been jealously handed down from the Collegia of ancient Rome, but both the brethren of the cloister, and the Masonic brethren were alike subject to the Chief Master Mason, who was an autocrat of the strictest type, and ruled over his masters, fellows, and apprentices with the despotism of a Cæsar.

How great and all-absorbing was the love for architecture in that period, and its influence in placing the Craft high in the estimation of the world may be realised when we read that the chief Master, dressed in the robes of his office, was a favoured guest at Court, and allowed precedence over nobles and warriors of renown. Charlemagne took direct and immediate interest in the work, in one of his palaces eleven apartments were set aside for workrooms and others for the storage of material.

As may be readily assumed, the architecture of that early period, employed both in Germany, France and England, was based with more or less variation on the round arch, the flat roof, and the double row of columns, which formed the leading features of the Roman basillica, such as we may see, for example, in Santa Maria, Maggiore, and San Giovanni Lateran, in Rome, the main divergence being chiefly noticeable in the short square tower with which the Saxon and

Norman ecclesiastical edifices were so conspicuously connected, having its origin as a strong place of refuge from turbulent and tempestuous persecutions.

In this era many notable cathedrals were erected in Germany. Among them may be quoted the Cathedral of Magdeburg, to which has been given the somewhat apocryphal date of 876 A.D. To carry out works of such magnitude, the services of a large number of men for several consecutive years would naturally be called for. To accommodate the artisans, booths or sheds of boards were built around the wall of the edifices under construction, and these, in the German language, were called Hütte—an equivalent to our English name of Lodge. In these Hütte the Masons kept their tools, assembled for work, and most probably ate and slept. They joined together in mutual help and encouragement; they had special signs of recognition—by some are believed to have had secret ceremonies; and were kept together by certain laws, to which they were bound by oath.

Among the earliest Masters of lodges will be found the name of Abbot Wilhelm von Hirschaw, Count Palatine of Scheuren, who, in 1080, was Master of the Lodge of St. Emmerau, in Ratisbon, and is by many accepted as the real founder of the German Bauhütten. Nor was it exceptional for the highest dignitaries to be found among the front ranks of the Masons. In 1090, a Master Mason was elevated to the rank of Bishop of Salzburg, and many other eminent names might readily be quoted.

THE STEINMETZEN'S INITIATION.

In Findel's "History of Freemasonry," the following account is given of the initiation of a candidate into the ancient Lodges of the Steinmetzen of Germany, and, from the many points of resemblance it contains to the work of a modern Lodge, it must be read with much interest by every member of the Craft. It is, however, only just to say that certain of the best accepted of our modern Masonic Historians do not give an implicit adherence to the authenticity of the account.

"A complete insight into the customs in use among the Fraternity of Stonemasons—into their origin and progress—will, most likely, never be vouchsafed to us. Nevertheless, we know enough to decide that in all essential particulars they were the product of German soil. Even the English Catechism, as preserved to us amongst the Sloane Manuscripts, No. 3329, contains passages referring to the ancient German Vehmic Courts (Vehme). We will leave undecided what Fallou asserts—that the form of initiation amongst the Stonemasons was an imitation of the rite of consecration of the Order of Benedictines.

"The Fellow Craft, when he had served his time, and was desirous of being admitted into the Fraternity, was obliged, as in other guilds, to prove that he was of respectable parentage, born in wedlock, and bore a good reputation (there were some trades which were thought dishonourable, and on that account their sons were ineligible as members of a Guild). Most of the statutes required expressly that they should be free-born—of blameless reputation—possessing capacity both of body and mind. The candidate then received his peculiar mark, which henceforward he had to cut into every work in which he was engaged. The Brother who proposed his admission had likewise to become security for his good conduct. On the day fixed, the candidate went into the house where the assemblies were held, where the Master of the chair had had everything prepared in due order in the hall of the Craft; the brethren were then summoned (of course, bearing no weapons of any kind, it being a place dedicated to Peace), and the Assembly was opened by the Master, who first acquainted them with the proposed inauguration of the candidate, despatching a brother to prepare him. The messenger, in imitation of an ancient heathen custom, suggested to his companion that he should assume the demeanour of a supplicant; he was then stripped of all weapons, and everything of metal taken from him; he was divested of half his garments, and with his eyes bound, and breast and left foot bare, he stood at the door of the hall, which was open to him after three distinct knocks. The Junior Warden conducted him to the Master, who made him kneel and repeat a prayer. The candidate was then led three times round the hall of the Guild, halting at last at the door, and putting his feet together in the form of a right angle, that he might in three upright square steps place himself in front of the Master. Between the two, lying open on the table, was a New Testament, a pair of compasses, and a Mason's square, over which, in pursuance of an ancient custom, he stretched out his right hand, swearing to be faithful to the duties to which he pledged himself, and to keep secret whatever had been or might be thereafter made known to him in that place.

"The bandage was then removed from his eyes, the three great Lights were shewn him, a new apron bound round him, the pass word given him, and his place in the hall of the Guild pointed out to him. The manner of knocking and the grip of the hand were, and are, the same as those now used by the Apprentices in Freemasonry. After the Master had enquired if anyone had anything else to submit to the decision of the assembly, he closed the proceedings with the usual knocks of the Stonemason's hammer.

"At the banquet which invariably succeeded the reception of the candidate, which feasts were always opened and closed with prayer, the chief Master proposed to drink the health of the newly-accepted brother, in the drinking called 'Willkommen,' to which the brother replied by drinking to the welfare of the whole Fraternity. At that time, as now, and in all other guilds, healths were drunk with three times three : the cup was taken hold of with a glove or pocket handkerchief, the cover lifted off, and, lastly, it was carried to the lips, and the cup was emptied in three draughts, and replaced on the table in three motions."

ORIGIN OF GOTHIC ARCHITECTURE.

With the crusades there came a vast change over the spirit of architecture. The unaccustomed designs that had been seen in the east awoke the imagination and fired the ambition of the French architects and builders, and from the germ thus grafted it is not unwarrantable to believe they produced those exquisite and graceful edifices that have since charmed and delighted the world. It must, however, be admitted that a natural tendency toward the pointed arch had previously began to exhibit itself. We have already noticed that the Romans took up the grand legacy of the Arch which had been left them by their Etrurian predecessors, and that from it they developed those magnificent monuments which still so nobly adorn and glorify the Eternal City. The special feature of the

Roman Arch may be roughly stated as a semi-circle surmounting two uprights, associated for the most part with straight walls and flat roofs, modelled chiefly on the principles of the architecture of Greece.

But, the round arch, though that in use in Rome, was not the only arch known to antiquity. The illustration (*Fig.* 3, *Plate* xv., *Page* 122) is taken from Rawlinson's " Five Monarchies," and represents a pointed Assyrian false arch. Arches of this type were spoken of in days of antiquity as the Greek Arch, and identically similar ones are to be seen both in Greece and Etruria. We have thus clear evidence that the pointed arch was in vogue centuries before the foundation of Rome. There can be no doubt that the ruins of such arches were familiar to the crusaders during their wanderings in the East, and it should be borne in mind that other than fighting men were in the ranks of their armies. The crusaders ever had before them the final occupation of the Holy Land, by Christian people, as their objective point, and castles of defence and other buildings were consequently erected by them. To this end large bodies of French and other Masons from the mediæval Guilds were called upon to take part, and, as will be found in the most admirable publications of the " Palestine Exploration Fund," Masons' marks are as thick in the Holy land as leaves in the Valambrosa.

Here, then, we have a very likely clue to what, in all probability, gave a great impetus to the so-called Gothic architecture, which made its first appearance in France about the middle of the twelfth century (1160). Bayet, in his valuable work—" Précis d'historie de l'art," says that it is an established fact that Gothic architecture first made its appearance in the Ile-de-France, and that the most ancient examples are the

Church of Noyon, the Cathedral of Sens, parts of the Church of St. Denis, Notre Dame de Chalons, Saint Remi de Reims, and others, several of which date back to the end of the twelfth century.

Nothing can be more remarkable than the change in art and manners which the Gothic art was destined to bring about. Following the grand, though well-worn type so long in use and in which the builders now found little outlet for the exercise of imagination beyond the elaborate sculpturing of porch and doorway, came the endless tracery and ceaseless ornament of the new art. Lofty arches reared the elegant grace of their pointed summits high in the air; the dim, sombre, and unpicturesque interior beneath the flat Roman roof gave way to floods of light streaming through great windows of gorgeously coloured glass, while the intricate interlacings of groined archings and the long vista of delicate columns grouped into massive supports, gave to the edifice a new charm and a romantic tone that was vividly appreciated, that led men's minds into fresh channels of thought, and was quickly imitated on all sides.

The illustration (*Fig.* 1, *Plate* xv.), taken from "The Gentleman's Magazine" for 1815, gives the outline of an arch in Westminster Abbey, built in 1245, having the proportions of three to one, and is a remarkable instance of the distinguishing peculiarity of early Gothic and its identical similitude to the "Greek arch" (*Fig.* 3, *Plate* xv.) of the ancient builders of Greece and Mesopotamia.

If they had not the honour of introducing it, the German Masons certainly lost no time in accepting the new art. Albertus Magnus, Count of Bollstädt, is

122   SYMBOLS AND LEGENDS OF FREEMASONRY.

reported to have designed Cologne Cathedral in 1249. Animated by his love of Masonry, Albertus Magnus gave a fresh impulse to the members of the Fraternity in Germany, and taught in their Lodges the mathematical rules and proportions on which the new style of architecture was constructed.

The secret Masonic alphabet by which instructions might be passed from one Lodge to another without fear of discovering them to those who were not numbered among the initiated has also by some been attributed to Albertus Magnus. The alphabet was composed wholly of geometric Masonic symbols, dots, and angles, and is said to have been in use among Masons in France down to the end of last century. *Fig.* 4, *Plate* xv., is the key to the principle on which the alphabet was contrived.

The year 1277 saw the commencement of the Strasburg Cathedral, which is now admitted to be one of the finest pieces of Gothic architecture existing. The architect was Ervin, of Steinbach, and Masons' marks are to be found in every part of the glorious edifice. Its solid foundations were so firmly laid, and its apparently fragile architecture so admirably constructed that, notwithstanding the flight of centuries and the shocks of storm and earthquake, the cathedral stands to-day perfect and true in all its exquisite beauty, an almost imperishable testimony to the excellence of the work and the soundness of the plans which distinguished the labours of the ancient fathers of the Craft.

FREEMASONS AND THE ROMAN CHURCH.

The intimacy between cleric and lay Masons was at this time still in vogue, and the Freemasons occupied

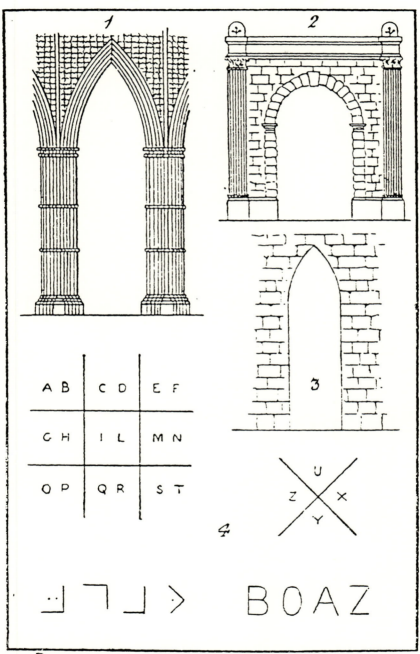

PLATE. XV.

a high place in Papal esteem. In 1278, as accepted tradition tells us, Pope Nicholas III. issued an indulgence to the Lodge of Strasburg which, for the excellence of its work, had merited his special approbation. It is, however, but right to state that, although this tradition has long been accepted, no documentary evidence in its support is known to exist. A little later on, the Masons of Strasburg, Vienna, Cologne, Zurich, and Friburgh formed themselves into a fraternity to which they gave the name of Hütten, and the brethren of these Lodges recognised Strasburg as the Haupt-Hütte—the High or Chief Lodge. On the 25th April, 1459, the chiefs of the united Lodges being assembled at Ratisbon drew up the Act of Fraternity and established the Master of the Lodge at Strasburg and his successors as Sole High or Chief Master of the Fraternity of Masons.

According to Findel the members of the confederation at Ratisbon consisted of Masters, Parlierers, and Journeymen. The Parlierer was an officer who represented the Master when his engagements prevented his being personally present. It was the Parlierer's duty to receive travelling brethren into the Hütte, see that they were provided with a fraternal reception, and given work if sought for or the needs of the Lodge required. It is interesting to note that this officer still holds place in Modern Masonry. In the Lodge in Rome an officer called the Orator sits beside the Master, and it is his duty to pronounce an oration on the advent of strangers and to speak upon topics which are brought under the notice of the Lodge. Findel says: "The word Polirer is a corruption of Parlierer—he who supplied the place of the Master in his absence and also addressed strangers." Parlier is a French word, signifying—a gossip. Bro. G. W. Speth, secretary to the Lodge Quatuor Coronati, contends that Findel is in error in thinking Polirer to be a corruption of Parlierer. He argues, and with every appearance of correctness, that the word is a German word, such as members of the German Fraternity might be well expected to use. "Old German courts of justice were held in the open air and surrounded by stakes like a prize ring. In Gothic a stake was called, *pal* ; modern German, *pfahl* ; English, *pale*. The warden of the Pale was the Palirer or Pfahlirer, incorrectly written Parlierer. Thus, we have the English word Warden as an equivalent of Parlirer."

The good terms which we have seen existed between the Church and the Fraternity at last, however, became much strained, the wrong doings which have been imputed to the ecclesiastics, and are said to have brought about the reformation of Luther, led to estrangement and finally to bitter feud between the clergy and the brethren of the Craft. Purity of living, and belief in the one Supreme Ruler, the Architect of the Universe, had ever been among the foremost of the tenets of Masonry, taught alike in the symbols of the Craft, and in the secret mysteries of initiation. That the gross sensualities which histories and traditions tell us were practised in many of the so-called religious houses, should be a matter of disgust and offence to the Masons may be readily comprehended. Nor, with the rude outspoken wit of the period, did they refrain from holding up to public execration the debauched life and dreary bewildering doctrine with which many of the ecclesiastics have been accredited. This, the following examples taken from Findel's "History of Freemasonry" abundantly prove :—

"In the St. Sebaldus Church, in Nuremburg, is a carving in stone, representing a nun in the lewd embrace of a monk. In the large Church in Strasburg, in one of the transepts opposite the pulpit, a hog and a goat may be seen carrying a sleeping fox as a sacred relic, a she dog is following the hog, in advance of the procession is a bear with a cross, and before the bear a wolf holding a burning wax taper. Then follows an ass reading mass at an altar. In the Cathedral at Würzburg, are to be found the significant columns Boaz and Jachin which were in the porch of King Solomon's Temple. In the Altar of the Church of Doberan in Mecklenburg, there are many triangles placed in a significant manner, there is also a well-preserved altar piece which shows the religious views of the Architects. In the foreground there are priests turning a mill grinding dogmatic doctrines therein. In the upper part of the picture is the Virgin Mary with the child Jesus, having a flaming star in the lower part of the body. At the bottom of the picture is a representation of the Lord's supper, in which the Apostles are placed in the well-known Masonic attitude. In the Cathedral of Brandenburg a fox in priestly robes is preaching to a flock of geese. In the Minster at Berne, in a picture of the Last Judgment, the Pope is represented amongst the damned."

It is, of course, much to be regretted that these old time Masons should have permitted themselves such licence of satire, and should have degraded the walls of stately edifices, constructed to embody the noblest thoughts which inspire the hearts of men, with the pitiful representation of the evil doings of unworthy churchmen. We must not, however, overlook the customs and manners of the times; no public press existed to throw light into the dark ways of noisome corners, no safeguards, like the caricatures of the modern journal, ridiculed public scandals and drove them abashed from the sight of men. Coarse and brutal means were those alone which were at their command. Bramante induced the Pope to have the nudity of Michael Angelo's frescoes hidden beneath extemporised folds of drapery. Not satisfied with dubbing his enemy "the breeches maker," Michael Angelo introduced a portrait of this hero of pudicity, decorated with a pair of Midian ears, into the lowest pit of hell in his celebrated painting of the Last Judgment, the crowning work of the Sixtine Chapel.

The Pope seems to have taken the joke in good part, and to have been amused at it rather than otherwise, for on Bramante's bringing a pitiful complaint of the indignity he had suffered, His Holiness with grim humour remarked that he regretted that it would be impossible for him to interfere, as the jurisdiction of the Holy See did not extend beyond the bounds of Purgatory, and that the region wherein Michael Angelo had placed him was altogether out of his control. Whatever authenticity may be attached to the anecdote, the libel still remains. Bramante's head and long ears are still to be seen encircled by the pictured tortures of the damned in a chapel which not a few look upon as something like the Holy of Holies, the central shrine of Christendom, handing down at once a comment on the coarseness of the age, and an unpleasant record of spiteful vindictiveness on the part of the great Michael Angelo himself.

ENGLAND.

THE LEGACY OF THE ROMAN MASONS.

Notice has already been made of the remains of Roman architecture found in various parts of England, many of which are still in existence, and reference to the possibility of our early forefathers having been admitted into the mysteries and initiated into the secrets of the Roman Colleges: but although the probability is great and the inference a fair and natural one, we have not even tradition to warrant us in setting forth that the ancient Britons were at that time members of the great Fraternity of Masons. Much that is indeed very plausible, and in all likelihood quite true, may be shown to connect the Celtic Druids with Masonry as we have followed it in the old world countries of the east. Their rock-built temples contained closely corresponding symbols, and their belief in the unity of the Creator, as opposed to a pantheon of idols, had certainly much in common with the underlying convictions of Freemasonry. But Stonehenge, the pyramids, and the sphinx are alike shrouded in the mists of an era either too remote or too inaccessible to be in any manner essayed within the limits of the present undertaking.

We do not even reach the surroundings of tradition, so far as English Masonry is concerned, till we arrive at the time of King Athelstan. To that period we find accredited a not improbable, but by no means well authenticated legend, which has been recorded as follows, by Anderson, in his "Constitution of Freemasonry," published in 1723.

AN ANCIENT LEGEND.

"But for the further instruction of candidates and younger brethren a certain record of Freemasons, written in the reign of King Edward IV., of the Norman line, gives the following account, viz. :—

"That though the ancient Records of the Brotherhood in England were many of them destroyed or lost in the Wars of the Saxons and Danes, yet King Athelstan (the grandson of King Alfred the Great, a mighty architect), the first anointed King of England, and who translated the Holy Bible into the Saxon Tongue, when he had brought the Land into Rest and Peace, built many great works, and encouraged many Masons from France, who were appointed Overseers thereof, and brought with them the Charges and Regulations of the Lodges preserved since the Roman times, who also prevailed with the King to improve the Constitution of the English Lodges according to the foreign Model, and to increase the wages of working Masons.

"That the said King's youngest son, Prince Edwin, being taught Masonry, and taking upon him the Charges of a Master Mason for the Love he had to the said Craft, and the honourable Principles whereon it is grounded, purchased a free Charter of King Athelstan, his Father, for the Masons having a Correction among themselves (as was anciently expressed), or a Freedom and Power to regulate themselves, to amend what might happen amiss, and to hold a yearly Communication and General Assembly.

"That accordingly Prince Edwin summoned all the Masons in the Realm to meet him in a Congregation at York, who came and composed a General Lodge, of which he was Grand Master ; and having brought with them all the Writings and Records extant, some in Greek, some in Latin, some in French, and other Languages, from the Contents thereof that Assembly did frame the Constitution and Charges of an English Lodge, made a Law to preserve and observe the same in all time coming, and ordained good Pay for working Masons, &c., &c.

"That in process of time, when Lodges were more frequent, the Right Worshipful the Master and Fellows, with Consent of the Lords of the Realm (for most great Men were then Masons), ordained that, for the future, at the Making and Admission of a Brother, the Constitution should be read, and the Charges hereunto annexed, by the Master or Warden, and that such as were to be admitted Master-Masons, or Masters of Work, should be examined whether they be able of Cunning to serve their respective Lords, as well the Lowest as the Highest, to the Honour and Worship of that aforesaid Art, and to the Profit of their Lords; for they be their Lords that employ and pay them for their Service and Travel."

And besides many other things, the said Record adds, "That those Charges and Laws of Freemasons have been seen and perused by our late Sovereign, King Henry VI., and by the Lords of his honourable Council, who have allowed them, and said that they be right, good, and reasonable to be holden, as they have been drawn out and collected from the Records of ancient Times."

The account thus given clearly purports to be nothing but tradition, and tradition, though of immense value in indicating the fact of the existence of a given original idea, presents us but too often with a distorted reflexion, a garbled and confused account of what was once a living and acting entity. But although many may cast doubts upon the veracity of the legend of Edwin and his Father (or Brother)

King Athelstan, a few years later both ample and unmistakable testimony was forthcoming to prove the existence of the great Masonic body in England, and to exhibit not only their skill in conquering inanimate nature, and welding from it the living shrines of exquisite beauty that so worthily adorn our land, but to show the high position of dignity and importance they held in the state.

MASONS' MARKS.

In the glorious cathedral at Gloucester, dating from 1089, Masons' marks are frequently found. Those who seek in the nave and on the first Norman pillar from the west end will find, if they have the secret teachings of Masonry to guide them, abundant proof to convince them that the hands of their Brethren were the contrivers and artificers of the magnificent pile above and around them. Melrose Abbey will, in like manner, give irrefutable testimony of a similar nature, dating from 1136. York Minster speaks with the self-same voice, and from a still more distant day.

Just a word concerning Masons' marks may be here advantageously introduced. It was a custom among Operative Masons that each individual artizan should have his special "mark," a signature to identify himself with his works. This mark, for the greater part, consisted of new arrangements of old geometric forms, which were peculiar to the Craft, reproducing in the main symbols of the greatest antiquity with such developments and variations as the skill or genius of the Craftsman might suggest. These marks are scattered broadly over the face of the architectural world; not in Europe alone, but also, as we have already seen, in endless variety among the numerous forts and Churches which the Crusaders erected in the Holy Land. We read, moreover, in "The Survey of Western Palestine," vol. v. p. 138—Greek Masons' marks are to be seen in the walls of the Temples at Baalbec.

ROYAL MASONS.

Continuing our *résumé*, we find that in 1202 the Bishop of Winchester established a company of Masons for extensive works on Winchester Cathedral, and the artificers have not failed to record their symbols in a conspicuous place in the carved stalls of the choir. In 1350, the word Freemason occurs for the first time in a public document, and may be seen in the twenty-fifth statute of Edward III. In 1420, in the reign of Henry VI., it is recorded that a body of Freemasons entered into a contract with the churchwardens of a parish in Suffolk, making it an express stipulation that they should be provided with a lodge properly "tiled" in which they could hold their meetings (*See Appendix, page* 2.) Elizabeth did not hold Freemasons in the highest esteem, her autocratic will was little able to brook a society of whose tenets she could obtain no knowledge, and in whose dealings she could interpose no authority. So incensed was the Royal Lady against the Craft, that in 1558 (according to an accepted tradition), she determined upon breaking up their meetings at York, and instructed Lord Sackville to carry out her commands. Lord Sackville, however, reported with such high encomiums on the scope and object of the Fraternity, that the Queen was induced to forego her intentions, and, though she never received the Craft into her favour, she left it unmolested during the remainder of her reign.

By the close of the century the Craft was in a firm

position, practising, not only operative, but speculative Masonry, as will be understood by the position of the following gentlemen who were admitted to the membership of the lodges. The roll of St. Mary's Lodge at Edinburgh, No. 1 of Scotland, sets forth that J. Boswell, Esq., of Auchinleck, attended that lodge in 1600. Robert Moray, Quartermaster-General of the army, was admitted to the mysteries of the Craft at the lodge in Newcastle, in the year 1641. This being the earliest mention of an initiation in England. We also learn that Elias Ashmole and Col. Henry Mainwaring were made Masons at Warrington, in Lancashire, in the year 1646.

A very loose and unreliable tradition has it that both James the First, and his grandson, Charles the Second, were " Free and Accepted Masons." Anderson, in his famous Master's song, sings : " . . . learned James, a mason king, who first of kings revived the style of great Augustus." But he fails to give any manner of authority for his assertion, beyond the fact that he was the great patron of Inigo Jones, and turns the point of his song by advising the company to fill their tankards and drink to the health of the Great Augustus, who, like " the Flaunting extravagant Quean " of later days, was, of course, well qualified to " prove an excuse for the glass."

But whether the " learned James," the amorous Charles, or the valiant Dutchman, who, also, as Anderson tells us, was " reckoned by most men to be a Mason," were really members of the Fraternity or not, is certainly not a matter of the very highest importance. Masons who are willing to accept Anderson's statements as they appear in his revised book of Constitutions, 1738, may console themselves by believing that Sir

Christopher Wren was a distinguished member of the Craft. But although Wren was one among the greatest architects that any country or any era has produced, and gratifying as it would be to substantiate Anderson's assertion, it is to be feared that the assumption stands on very doubtful ground. No documentary evidence of any kind attests it, and as will be seen by a careful perusal of Gould's "History of Freemasonry," where the subject has received a thorough and exhaustive consideration, the best that may be said concerning Sir Christopher Wren's connection with Freemasonry is, that it is unproved, and yet remains an open question.

The testimony of the progress of Masonry in England in the olden days is to be found published in other books, at far greater length, and in far greater detail than has been attempted here, notably in the works of Hughan and Gould : but, sufficient has been shown to indicate the undeniable fact that a body of men, here, as on the continent of Europe, and in the bygone days of antiquity, were banded together for the double purpose of accepting and understanding certain traditional mysteries, and aiding and supporting each other in carrying out and demonstrating the truths of science, and in developing the higher branches of the arts.

With the unhappy reign of James II. a blight seemed to settle on all the nobler faculties of the nation, our Universities were degraded to the meanest of scholars. The gross corruption of literature which set in under Charles II. and the Restoration dragged all that was elevated, pure, and beautiful into the common sewer of the gutter, and the bitter persecution that throve on the audacious lies of men like Oates and Bedloe drove Freemasonry to the wall and left but the merest

134 SYMBOLS AND LEGENDS OF FREEMASONRY.

traces of it to linger through an evil and uncertain existence. How the threads of these traces were gathered together in a less forbidding time and the foundations of modern Freemasonry fixed, will shortly be considered, and we now take leave of the record of Ancient Masonry by quoting the great Legend of Freemasonry as it is to be found in "The Gentleman's Magazine" for June, 1815, and also referring, among many others of undoubted authenticity, to an ancient manuscript of close similarity, which is still in existence and is known as the Wilson MS. According to the Rev. A. F. A. Woodford, who published an account and a *fac simile* of the manuscript in 1878, it dates from 1650, and has probably been copied from a manuscript of much older date, and was, at the time of publishing his book, in the possession of the Rev. J. E. A. Fenwick, of Cheltenham. For those desirous of further knowledge of the old MSS. the fullest possible information will be found in the works of Gould and Hughan.

The transcript from the "Gentleman's Magazine" should be read with care, because, as will afterwards be seen, the legend therein contained forms in no small degree the foundation upon which Modern Freemasonry has been modelled.

Copied from the "Gentleman's Magazine," 1815. p. 489:—

"For the gratification of your readers, I send you a curious address respecting Freemasonry, which not long since came into my possession. It is written on a roll of parchment, in a very clear hand, apparently early in the 17th century, and very probably is copied from a MS. of earlier date.—Yours, &c., JAMES DOULAND.

THE ENGLISH TRADITION.

"'The might of the Father of Kings, and the wisdome of his glorious grace through the goodness of the Holy Ghost, there bene three Persons in one Godheade, be with us at the beginninge, and give us grace so to governe us here in this mortall liveinge, that we may come to his Kingdome that never shall have endinge. Amen.

"'Good Bretheren and Fellowes, our purpose is to tell you how and in what manner this worthy science of Masonrye was begunne, and afterwards how it was favoured by worthy Kings and Princes, and by many other worshippfull men. And also, to those that be willinge, wee will declare the charge that belongeth to any true Mason to keepe for in good faith. And yee, have good heede thereto; it is well worthy to be well kept for a worthy Craft and a curious science. For there be seaven liberall Sciences, of the which seaven it is one of them. And the names of the seaven Scyences bene these:—First is Grammare; and it teacheth man to speake truely and write truely. And the second is Rethoric; and teacheth a man to speake faire in subtill tearmes. And the third Dialectyke; and that teacheth a man for to discerne or know truth from false. And the fourth is Arithmeticke; and that teacheth man for to reckon and to accompte all manner of numbers. And the fifth is called Geometrie; and that teacheth mett and measure of earth, and of all other things; of the which science is called Masonrye. And the sixt science is called Musicke; and that teacheth a man of songe and voice, of tongue and orgaine, harpe and trompe. And the seaventh science is called Astromomye; and that teacheth a man the course of the sunn, moone, and starrs. These be the seaven liberall sciences, the which been all founded by one science; that is to say, Geometrie. And this may a man prove, that the science of the worke is founded by Geometrie, for Geometrie teacheth a man mett and measure, ponderation and weights all manner of things on earth; for there is noe man that worketh any science but he worketh by some mett or some measure, nor noe man that buyeth or selleth but he buyeth or selleth by some measure or by some weight, and all these is Geometrie. And these merchants and all Craftsmen, and all other of the seaven sciences, and in especially the plowman and tillers of all manner of grounds graynes, seedes, vynes, plowers and sellers of other fruits: for Grammer or Retricke, neither Astronomie nor none of all the other seaven sciences, can noe manner find mett nor measure without Geometrie. Wherefore methinketh that the science of Geometrie is most worthy, and that findeth all other.

"'How that these worthy sciences were first begoune, I shall tell you. Before Noyes flood the was a man called Lameche, as it is written in the Byble in the iiijth chapter of Genesis: and this Lameche had two wives, and the one height Ada and the other height Sella: by his first wife Ada he got two Sonns, and that one Jahell, and the other Tuball. And by that other wife Sella he gott a son and a daughter. And these four children founden the beginning of all sciences in the world. And this ilder son Jahell found the science of Geometrie, and he departed flocks of sheepe and lands in the field, and first wrought house of stone and tree, as it is noted in the chapter above said. And his brother Tuball found the science of Musicke, songe of tonge, harpe and orgaine. And the third brother Tubal Cain found Smith-craft of gold, silver, copper, iron and steele; and the daughter found the craft of weavinge. And these children knew well that God would take vengeance for synn, either by fire or by water, wherefore they writt their science that they had found in two pillars of stone, that they might be found after Noyes flood. And that one stone was marble, for that would not bren with fire. And that other stone was clipped laterns, and would not drown in noe water.

Our intent is to tell you trulie how and in what manner these stones were found that thise science were written in the great Hermarynes that was Cubys son. The which Cub was Lem's son, and that was Noy's son. This Hermarynes afterwards was called Harmes, the father of wise men; he found one of the two pillars of stone, and found the science written there, and he taught it to other men. And at the making of the tower of Babylon there was Masonry first made much of. And the King of Babylon that height Nemrothe, was a mason himselfe; and he loved well the science, as it is said with masters of histories. And when the city of Nyneve, and other cities of the east should be made, Menrothe, the King of Babylon send thither threescore Masons at the rogation of the King of Nyneve his cosen. And when he sent them forth, he gave them a charge on this manner. That they should be true each of them to other, and that they should love truly together, and that they should serve their lord truly for their pay; soe that the master may have worshipp, and all that long to him. And other moe charges he gave them. And this was the first time that ever Mason had any charge of his science.

"'Moreover, when Abraham and Sara his wife went into Egypt, there he taught the seaven scyences a comission that I may have power to rule them after the manner that the sciences ought to be ruled. And that the King and all his councell granted to him anone, and sealed their commission. And then this worthy doctor woke to him those lords sonns and taught them the science of Geometrie in praetise, for to worke in stones all manner of worthy worke that belongeth to buildinge churches, temples, castells, towres and manners, and all other manner of buildings; and he gave them a charge on this manner.

"' The first was, that they should be true to the King, and to the Lord that they owe. And that they should love well together, and be true each one to the other. And that they should call each other his fellowe, or else brother, and not by servant, or his knave, nor none other foule name. And that truly the should deserve their paie of the lord, or of the master that they serve. And that they should ordaine the wisest of them to be master of the worke ; and neither of love nor great lynneadge ritches ne for noe favour to tell another that hath little couning for to be master of the lord's worke, where through the lord should be evill served and they ashamed. And also that they should call their governors of the worke Master, in the time that they worke with him. And other many moe charges that longe to tell. And to all these charges he made them to sweare a great oath that men used in that time ; or ordayned for them reasonable wages, that they might live honestly by. And also that they should come and semble together every yeare once, how they might worke best to serve the lord for his profitt, and to their owne worshipp ; and to correct within themselves him that had trespassed against the science. And thus was the science grounded there ; and that worthy Mr. Euclide gave it the name of Geometrie, And now it is called through all this land Masonrye.

"'Sythen long after, when the children of Israell were coming into the land of Beheast, that is now called amongst us the Country of Jhrlm. Kinge David began the temple that they called Templum D'ni, and it is named with us the temple of Jerusalem. And the same King David loved Masons well, and cherished them much, and gave them good paie. And he gave the charges and the manners as he had learned of Egypt, given by Euclide, and other charges moe, that yee shall heare afterward. And after the decease of King David, Salamon, that was David's sonn, performed out the Temple that his father begonne; and sent after Masons into divers countries and of divers lands, and gathered them together so that he had forescore thousand workers of stone, and were all named Masons. And he choose out of them three thousand that were ordayned to be Maisters and governors of his worke. And furthermore, there was a Kinge of another region that men called Iram, and he loved well Kinge Solomon, and he gave him tymber to his worke. And he had a sonn that height Aynon, and he was a master of Geometrie, and was chiefe Maister of all his Masons, and was Master of all his gravings and carvinge, and of all other manner of Masonrie that longed to the Temple; and this is wittnessed by the Bible, in libro Regum the third chapter. And this Solomon confirmed both charges and the manners that his father had given to Masons. And this was that worthy science of Masonrye confirmed in the Country of Jerusalem, and in many other Kingdomes.

"'Curious Craftsmen walked about full wide into divers countryes, some because of learninge more craft and cuninge, and some to teach them that had but little conynge. And soe it befell that there was one curious Mason that height Maymas Grecus, that had been at the making of Solomon's Temple, and he came to France, and there was one of the Regal lyne of Frannce that height Charles Martell; and he was a man that loved well such a science, and drew to this Maymus Grecus that is aforesaid and learned of him the science, and tooke upon him the charges and manners; and afterward by the grace of God he was elect to be Kinge of France. And when he was in his estate he tooke Masons, and did helpe to make men Masons that were none; and set them to worke, and gave them both the charge and the manners and good paie, as he had learned of other Masons; and confirmed them a Charter from yeare to yeare to hold their semble where they would; and cherished them right much. And thus came the science into France.

"'England is all this season stood voyd for any charge of Maysonrye into St. Albones tyme. And in his days the Kinge of England that was a Pagan, he did wall the towne about that is called Saicnt Albone. And Saicnt Albones was a worthy Knight, and steward with the Kinge of his household, and had governance of the realm, and also of the making of the towne walls; and loved well Masons, and cherished them much. And he made their paie right good, standinge as the realm did: for he gave them ijs. vjd. a week, and iiijd. to their nonesynehes. And before that time, through all this land, a Mason tooke but a penny a day and his meate, till Saicnte Albone amended it, and gave them a Chartour of the King and his councell for to hold a genellal councell, and gave it the name of Assemble; and thereat he was himselfe, and helped to make Masons, and gave them charges as you shall heare afterward.

"' Right soone after the decease of Saient Albone there came divers warrs into the realme of England of divers nations, soe that the good rule of Masonry was destroyed into the time of Kinge Athelstone dayes that was a worthy Kinge of England, and brought this land good rest and peace; and builded many great works of Abbeyes and Towres and other many divers buildings: and loved well Masons. And he had a sonne that height Edwinne, and he loved Masons much more than his father did. And he was a great practiser in Geometry, and he drew him much to talke and commune with Masons, and to learn of them science: and afterward for love that he had to Masons, and to the science, he was made Mason, and gatt of the Kinge his father a Chartour and Commission to hold every yeare once an assemble, wher that ever they would, within the realme of England; and to correct within themselves defaults and trespasses that were done within the science. And he held himselfe an Assemble at Yorke, and there he made Masons, and gave them charges, and taught them the manners, and commanded that rule to be kept ever after, and tooke then the Chartour and the Commission to keepe and made ordinance that it should be renewed from Kinge to Kinge.

"'And when the Assemble was gathered, he made a cry that all old Masons and young that had any writinge or understanding of the charges and the manners that were made before in this land or in any other, that they should shew them forth. And when it was proved, there was some founden in Frenche, and some in Greek; and some in English, and some in other languages; and the intent of them all was founden all one. And he did make a booke thereof, and how the science was founded. And he himselfe bad and commanded that it should be readd or tould, when that any Mason should be made, for to give him his charge. And fro that day unto this tyme manners of Masons have beene kept in that forme as well as men might governe it. And furthermore divers Assemblies have beene put and ordayned certain charges by the best advice of Masters and fellowes. *Tunc unus ex senioribus teneat librum, ut illi vel ille ponant vel ponat maines super librum: et tunc præcepta deberent legi.*

"'Every man that is a man take right good heed to these charges, if that any man find himselfe guilty in any of these charges, that he amend himselfe against God. And in principall, yee that been to be charged, take good heed that ye may keepe these charges right well, for it is great perill a man to forsweare himselfe upon a booke.

"'The first charge is, that he or thou shall be true man to God and Holy Church, and that he use neither error nor herysie by your understandinge or discreet men or wise men's teachinge. And also that he shall be true liege-man to the Kinge of England without treason or any other falsehood; and that they know no treason ne trechery, but if ye amend it privily if ye may, or else warn the Kinge or his councell. And also ye shal be true each one to other (that is to say) to every Mason of the science of Masonrye that bene Masons allowed, yee shall doe to them as ye would that they should doe to you; and also that yee keepe truly all the councells of Lodge and Chamber, and all other councells that ought to be kept of way of Masonhood.

And also that noe Mason shal be in thefte noe theevishe for as far forth as he may weete or know. And also that ye shal be true to the lord or master that ye serve, and truly see his profit and his advantage. And also ye shall call Masons your Brethren, or else your Fellowes, and none other foule names. And also yee shall not take your fellowe's wife in villany, nor desire ungodly his daughter nor his servant, nor put him to noe disworshipp. And also that yee pay truly for your meat and drinke there ye go to boarde. And also ye shall do no villany in that place where yee go to board, whereby the science might be slandered thereby. These be the charges in generall that belongeth to every true Mason to keepe Masters and Fellowes.

"' Rehearse I will, now, other charges singular for Masters and Fellows. First that no Master shall not take upon him noe lord's worke nor none other man's worke but hee know himself able and sufficient of cuninge to performe and end the lord's worke, soe that the science have noe slander nor noe disworshipp, but that the lord may be well served and truly. And also that noe Master take noe worke, but that he take it reasonable, soe that the lord may be truly served with his owne good, and the master to live honestly, and to pay his fellowes truly their paie as the manner is: And also that noe master ne fellowe shall not supplant other of their worke (that is to say) And ye have taken a worke, or else stand maister of the lord's worke, yee shall not putt him out but if he be unable of conynge for to end the worke. And also that noe master nor noe fellowe take noe apprentice within the terme of seaven yeares ; and that the apprentice be able of birth free-borne, and of lymes whole as a man ought to be : And also that noe maister nor fellowe take noe allowance to be made Mason without the assent and the councell of his fellowes at the least sixe or seaven given yeares; and he that shal be made Mason to be able in all manner of degrees (that is to say) free borne, and of good kindred come, and true and noe bondman: And also that noe Mason shall not take noe apprentice but if he have sufficient occupacion for to occupie on two fellowes or else three at the least: And also that noe Maister nor fellowe put noe lord's worke to taske that was want to goe to jornaye. And also that every master shall give paye to his fellowes but as he may deserve, so that yee be not deceived by false workmen: And also none of you slander another behind his back, to make him to loose his good name or his worldly goods: And also that no fellowe within the lodge or without misanswer eyther ungodly or reprovably without reasonable cause. And also that every Mason shall reverence his elder, and put him to worshippe: And also that no Mason shall not be any common player a hazard or at the dice, nor at any other unlawfull playes whereby the science might be slandered. And also that noe Mason shall not use noe lecherye, nor be noe bawde, whereby the science might be slandered. And also that noe fellowe goe into the towne on nights tyme there as a lodg is of fellowes, without that he have a fellowe with him that he may beare him wittnesse that he was in an honest place. And also that every master and fellow shall come th' Assemble, and it be within fifty myles about him, if he have any writeings. And if yee have trespassed against the science, for to abide the award of masters and fellowes, and to make them accorded if they may, and if they may not accord them, to go to the common lawe. And also that noe maister ne fellowe make noe molde nor squyar nor rule to noe layer, nor at noe layer within the lodge, nor without to hew noe molde stones. And also that every Mason receive and cherish strange fellowes when they come over the countryes, and set them a worke and they will as the manner is (that is to say) yf we have noe mould stones in his place, he shall refresh him with money into the next lodge. And also that every Mason shall truly serve the lord for his paie, and every master truly make an end of his worke be it taske or journey, if yee ought for to have. These charges that wee now rehearsed to you and to all other that belongeth to Masons, yee shall keepe, soe helpe you God, And your holy dome, and by this booke, unto your power. Amen."

MODERN FREEMASONRY.

THE LAST GREAT LINK WELDED.

The early part of last century might well have been called the age of lead—a universal dulness like a cloud of blight spread itself over the land; learning was at a low ebb; ignorance and stupidity prevailed even in the highest places. Robert Walpole, who made himself ruler over England during the reigns of the first and second Georges, might wrest a quotation or so from Horace, but knew almost nothing of one of the chief studies of a statesman—the study of history. Literature and her ministrants were in a sad plight; there was no medium between splendour and penurious squalor. An author was either a dandified gentleman and a Secretary of State, or "a poor miserable hack, slinking about the gin cellars and tripe shops, and huddling at night under a scanty coverlet in the attic of a Grub-street den." Such men as Swift, Steele, Addison, and, above all, the immortal Newton, shone like bright stars in the abyss of night; but they were isolated and lone, their fellow countrymen had not even the wit to raise them into a fashion. Happily, individual freedom under the new dynasty was fairly well assured, and men to a great extent might go about their own affairs without fear of spies, without the let or hindrance of those in authority over them. In this era Modern Freemasonry had its birth.

On the twenty-fourth of June, 1717, the Masonic Lodges of London, which had lived through the persecutions of James II., and the shiftless, restless, inane times that followed them, met together at the Apple Tree Tavern, and founded the now-existing Grand Lodge of England. Those who led the movement, moulded it into shape, and gave it the form in which we now find it, were a Scotch Divine, the Rev. James A. Anderson, D.D., and the Rev. J. Theophilus Desaguliers, chaplain to the Duke of Chandos, the first being responsible for the literary work of collecting the old legends of the Craft, preparing its ritual, and drawing up the Constitution and Charges, while the latter appears to have brought the Fraternity into vogue among the higher ranks of social life and to have enlisted their co-operation and sympathy.

Desaguliers was by birth a Frenchman, but became a fully naturalized citizen of the country in which the principal part of his life was spent. He was born at Rochelle in the year 1683, but was brought to England in early childhood. His education was a liberal one, for on entering life he soon became a distinguished writer, was a Fellow of the Royal Society, and, in 1713, was made M.A. at Christ Church, Oxford; he was also a lecturer on experimental philosophy, chaplain to the Duke of Chandos, and enjoyed the friendship of

Sir Isaac Newton. Mackenzie, in "The Royal Masonic Encyclopædia," says that he was initiated into the mysteries of Freemasonry in the Lodge held at "The Goose and Gridiron," which afterwards became known and celebrated as "The Lodge of Antiquity." It is now, however, shown by Gould that "Both Desaguliers and Payne were members in 1723 of the Lodge held at the Horn Tavern, in New Palace Yard, Westminster, which is described in the 'Constitutions' of 1738 as the old Lodge removed from the 'Rummer and Grapes,' Channel Row, whose constitution is immemorial."

Mackenzie states that after repeated conferences with the aged Sir Christopher Wren, Desaguliers obtained a meeting of the four London Lodges in 1717, which took place at the Apple Tree Tavern, when the Grand Lodge was constituted, and Anthony Sayer was elected first Grand Master. Modern authorities consider that the assumptions of Mackenzie and Findel on this matter can no longer be accepted as they are unsupported by any reliable evidence, and incline to the opinion that neither Wren, Desaguliers, nor Anderson had anything whatever to do with the events of 1716-17. We, however, know that two years later the exalted position of Grand Master was conferred on Desaguliers himself. From that time the Fraternity rapidly increased in numbers and influence, many noblemen and leading spirits of the day taking part in the ceremonies.

THE CONSTITUTIONS OF 1723.

In 1723 Anderson prepared and published his great work "The Constitution of the Freemasons," containing the history, charges, regulations, &c., of the Fraternity, and it was dedicated by Desaguliers, in his position of

Deputy Grand Master, to the Duke of Montagu, who then filled the office of Grand Master of England.

Anderson was a native of Scotland, said to have been born in Aberdeen, and was for many years minister of the Scotch Presbyterian Church, in Swallow-street, Piccadilly; he was a man of fair attainments for the time he lived in, but his literary productions, so far as they appear in Freemasonry, are more remarkable for the fertility of their imagination than the reliability of their data, or the accuracy of their statements. The history of Freemasonry which he gives us is evidently compiled out of Bible reading and the old Masonic legends which have just been quoted. It commences with Adam and wearily wends its way through a very devious and by no means authentic history of Architecture, in which assertion is vividly prominent on every hand and as vividly unsupported by data or testimony on which any manner of reliability may be placed.

After the charge and general regulations to be observed by Freemasons, Anderson winds up his book with Master and Warden songs, giving rhymed versions of the matter that has already appeared in the text of his work. These songs, although in the weakest of doggerel and trashy to the last degree, are of much interest in throwing light on the manners of life in that period, and for giving us a key to understand the various forces that had been at work in the contrivances of the ritual of Modern Freemasonry and the establishment of the doctrine it was intended to convey.

We may note in the first place with regard to the religious aspect of the newly re-constituted Fraternity, that, although the leading "craftsmen" were ministers of two strongly opposed religious sects, no importation of dogma was in any way introduced. Calvin and Knox, Episcopacy, and even Rome itself made no appearance whatever, neither in approbation nor in disfavour—the volume of Holy Writ was received with every token of respect and veneration; but the great primal tenet of all true Freemasonry, the unity of God, a fixed unswerving adherence to the Great Architect of the Universe, the creator and preserver of all things, never failed in striking the true key note of the Craft, never failed in adding its deep inherent testimony to that remote antiquity which, as we have already shown, began in the far-off early life of the world.

THE COMPILATION OF THE RITUAL.

With the knowledge of the character and attainments of Anderson and Desaguliers, which is easily to be obtained in the works they have left us, we have much that is valuable to guide us in tracing back to their origin many of the customs and observances of Modern Freemasonry: but we must never lose sight of the fact that into whatever form they may have cast the practices of Masonry, the forms themselves were based on traditions that had been held from antiquity. Thus, although we find Solomon's Temple placed in the forefront, it is not alone because the authors found it so palpably suggested to them in Bacon's "New Atlantis," in the Bible, in the Talmud, and in the writings of Josephus. Something from each of these sources was no doubt superadded to the original legend; but King Solomon's Temple had ever been one of the central themes of the Craft, and we have already seen how through the Middle Ages it remained prominently in view and was held in the highest estimation.

It is, of course, quite possible that an inventive genius, possessed of no higher antiquarian lore than might be compassed in the Latin, Greek, and Hebrew of these two divines, might have mapped out rites like those of the first and second Degrees of Freemasonry. Virgil and Apuleius were readily accessible, and if the hieroglyphics and the cuneiform inscriptions were as yet enigmas, and mortal hand had not as yet raised the veil of Isis, the road of Demeter when in search of Persephone was a palpable vehicle for ceremonial observance, and the set questions of the Hierophant offered a suggestively convenient origin for the ritual of the Lodge. But long before Anderson, Desaguliers, and Modern Freemasonry made their several entrances into the world a very similar ceremonial is reported, though, alas, not on very trustworthy foundation, to have been entertained by the Craft on the Continent, as we found during our researches into Masonry in Germany. To credit these men with producing the entire scene and theatre of the Lodge as a piece of whole cloth of their own manufacture is as outrageous as it is improbable.

No comment and no apology for the symbols of Masonry are needed ; that they are no inventions of the 18th century is a fact so plainly written on the face of history that neither argument nor assertion is called for—their proof lies in the unbroken chain of their own existence. That secret societies have existed in all ages of the world, having in view a simple belief in the Primary Cause, under whatever name it may be called, and holding, with the Egyptians, that that Primary Cause is the "obscurity beyond all knowledge," is proved in every history that has been handed down to us. It is equally true that none but the highest minds were enabled to accept such teachings, and that to lay them before the untaught and untrained would have ended in the irretrievable ruin of nations, in anarchy of the worst type, and a return to the old chaotic days when might alone was right.

Such coteries of men of high intellect and wide toleration we see beneath the mysteries of Osiris, beneath the mysteries of Eleusis, "where all instruction ends," in the Masonic Lodge of Pompeii, in the early days of the Church, in the calm of the cloisters during the days of their purity, and beneath the traditions clinging to the Mediæval Guilds of France, Germany, and our own country. Ever fostering and encouraging the useful arts of life, Freemasonry and its great exponents walked side by side with the undying, unchangeable truth conveyed in the one God as distinct from idols of wood and stone, from the works of man's hands, from hero worship, or from any attribute of earth or the surrounding universe.

SNEERS OF "SUN WORSHIP" REFUTED.

Such, then, we may clearly see, were the materials with which Anderson and Desaguliers had to deal; the tenets they had to handle were none of their own manufacture; they were somewhat foreign, indeed, in the breadth of their scope to the avocations of the daily life of these men, but it was their province to bring them together as the backbone of the constitution they had to construct, and, as a far mightier power than they was behind them, they succeeded well in their work, and have left as a monument, firm and unbroken, the main features of their task. Shallow and unlearned men, who are unable to look beneath the symbol and the allegory and discover the imperishable truths beyond them, have often thought that by pointing with scorn to the sun in splendour, and by flinging a cheap sneer in the phrase " Sun worshippers," they have brought a formidable accusation against Freemasonry. Let them read the following quotations from the Holy Scripture and they will soon discover the folly into which their sneers have betrayed them :—

" In the heavens hath he set a tabernacle for the sun."—Psalm xix., 4.

" For the Lord God is a sun and a shield."—Psalm lxxxiv., 11.

" Jesus was transfigured before them, and his face did shine like the sun."—Matthew xvii., 2.

" His countenance was as the sun."—Rev. i., 16.

Such references are scattered freely on the pages of Holy Writ, and neither Jew nor Christian confounds the symbol with the Deity any more than the Freemason confounds the sun in splendour with the Great Architect of the Universe, whose unseeable existence it typifies in physical and tangible form.

THE LEGEND OF HIRAM ABIF.

It now remains for us to turn our attention to that most difficult and tangled skein, the Legend of Hiram Abif. Gould, whose three handsome volumes constitute a most perfect Masonic library, and one which should be in possession of every Lodge in the country, tells us, when referring to another well-known secret society of Middle Ages, the Companionage, that with them, as with the Freemasons, the mutual acceptance of a Hiramic legend existed from a very remote period. As might well be expected the legend has passed through the long ages from the Roman colleges and the Pompeian Lodge to the foundation of Modern

Masonry, leaving but the faintest traces of its existence visible to the outside world. But the legend was the great truth on which the Mason's character was formed; it bore down to him the living message from Egypt, from Greece, from Rome, that whatever sophists might teach him, or whatever might be the allurements of false and transitory gods, the great eternal truths of life, death, and the hope of immortality had stood firm and unshaken for ages, and remained for ever the same—yesterday, to-day, and to-morrow.

What, then, must be our feelings when we first seek to analyse the legend to find that it apparently drops to pieces in our fingers and is withered at a breath.

The Bible tells us in the most direct language that Hiram did not leave the work of the Temple incomplete: in the first Book of Kings, chap. vii., ver. 40, we read, "So Hiram made an end of doing all the work that he had made for King Solomon for the house of the Lord." So circumstantial and so elaborate is the Scripture on all points connected with the building of the Temple that no manner of argument can set aside the fact that Hiram did finish the work in the Temple, and that the account set forth in the legend that he was treacherously murdered before even the completion of the stonework of the Temple, and that by his death one of the most important devices of operative masonry was nearly lost to the world—*is incorrect*.

Nevertheless, the Hiramic legend has a long descent, and if we carefully follow it up we may perhaps come to some clearer view than the mutilated form of it possessed by Anderson and Desaguliers. If we continue our search, we shall find that Hiram is called (by Masons) Hiram Abif. There is apparently no warranty for that name in the Bible. We there find him spoken of in one place as Huram, and in another, as Hiram. In the Wycliffe Bible he is called Yram, Iram and Hiram. Josephus corrupts the name into Chiram, or, as some have contended, returned it to its original Chaldean form. Yet, Masonic tradition hands us down Hiram Abif. Anderson affords proof to that fact in the note to his celebrated Charge. Hiram Abif, moreover, is one of the earliest names we find in Modern Freemasonry, thus, according to Findel's history, we learn that in 1721 Dr. John Beal was invested and installed by Bro. Payne in the chair of Hiram Abif to the left of the Grand Master. The authors of the Constitution were evidently puzzled to account for the name which tradition had brought down to them, hence the following note to *page* 11 of Anderson's "Constitutions" (1723):—"We read (2 Chron. ii., 13), Hiram, King of Tyre (called there Huram), in his Letter to King Solomon, says: 'I have sent a cunning man' (le Huram Abhi): not to be translated according to the vulgar Greek and Latin— Huram, my Father, as if this Architect was King Huram's Father; for his Description (*ver.* iv.) refutes it, and the Original plainly imports, Huram, of my Father's, viz.: the Chief Master Mason of my Father, King Abibalus (who enlarg'd and beautifi'd the City of Tyre, as ancient Histories inform us, whereby the Tyrians at this time were most expert in Masonry); though some think Hiram the King might call Hiram the Architect, Father, as learned and skilful Men were wont to be call'd of old Times, or as Joseph was called the Father of Pharoah; and as the same Hiram is call'd Solomon's Father (2 Chron. iv. 16) where 'tis said, *Shelomoh lammelech Abhif Churam ghnafah*—Did Huram, his Father, make to King Solomon. But the difficulty is over at once by allowing the Word Abif to be the Surname of Hiram the Mason, called also (Chap. ii. 13) Hiram Abi, as here Hiram Abif; for being so amply describ'd (Chap. ii. 14) we may easily suppose his Surname would not be conceal'd. And this Reading makes the Sense plain and complete, viz. : that Hiram, King of Tyre, sent to King Solomon his Namesake Hiram Abif, the Prince of Architects."

THE ANTIQUITY OF THE LEGEND.

If the latter part of the argument goes a little too far, and, on the principle of " Methinks the lady proves too much," rather damages our faith in what precedes it, it nevertheless leaves us in possession of the fact that Anderson found the name in existence, and sought with a skill well within the compass of his clerical office to explain it upon scriptural grounds. Gould, in his " History of Freemasonry," writing concerning Masonry in France, under the heading of " The Companionage," says : "To all the societies the connection of the Stonemasons with Hiram appears to have been known, and in some the members habitually wore white gloves, giving as a reason that they did so in order to testify their innocence in his death." He further says : " The Legend of Hiram the builder is not only anterior to 1726, the date of the introduction of Freemasonry into France, but probably coeval with the Companionage itself." Again : "We are driven to the conclusion that the 'Sons of Solomon,' as opposed to the 'Sons of Jacques,' certainly existed as early as 1640, and inferentially before A.D. 1400. I think we may at least safely conclude that their distinctive legend is of prior date to the introduction of Modern Freemasonry into France."

Wherever the Legend came from, it is, at all events, tolerably clear that it was in existence before 1717. Certainly, not even the most unscrupulous adventurer would have offered to the scrutiny of two notable divines an original story that on the very face of it clashed with the records of Scripture. We might, indeed, look with some misgivings upon its antiquity if it fitted into the story of Holy Writ and neatly dovetailed all its parts into the unimpeachable recorded history. Traditions have strange vagaries of their own, much handling works vast changes in them, sometimes they get a deep embroidery and a new dye from the complexion of the times they pass through, sometimes two traditions run colaterally, then the two fuse, and after a while the origins of both are lost or get so jumbled up that the clue to the starting point has ravelled out into a few doubtful and half-obliterated threads.

A CLUE TO ITS ORIGIN.

There are two such threads to be found in the Hiramic legend—the three murderers and the sprig of acacia. Let us see where they will lead us.

One of the search party on rising from the ground where he had been resting after his fatigues in seeking the missing Grand Master, pulled up with him from the earth a small sprig of acacia that was found to mark the burial place of the murdered Hiram. This thread leads several ways. First, the acacia is a shrub or small tree that grows abundantly in Palestine, and though held in great sanctity and frequently used in the East to mark their places of burial, was little likely to suggest itself as a botanic corroboration to any ingenious myth concocter at the beginning of the 18th century; it is a piece of local colouring that is far more probably an accompaniment of tradition than the cunning feature of an inventor. Virgil helps us to a second path to which this clue directs. It was a sprig, a golden bough, that the Cumean Sybil advised Æneas to present to Proserpine as an "open sesame" to the shadows of Hades. Nor was this the only adventure which occurred to Æneas in which a small sprig or shrub connects the living with the dead. "Priam, king of Troy, in the beginning of the Trojan war, committed his son Polydorus to the care of Polymester, king of Trace, and sent him a great sum of money. But after Troy was taken, the Thracian, for the sake of the money, killed the young prince and privately buried him. Æneas coming into that country, and accidentally plucking up a shrub that was near him on the side of a hill, discovered the murdered body of Polydorus." This is certainly a very close parallel, and might well have served the turn of the ingenious myth-builder; it, however, sadly lacks the local colouring of the acacia.

A third way takes in the murdered body of Osiris that was found in a shrub or tree of tamarisk not very far from where tradition finds the murdered body of Hiram Abif. The tamarisk is an attractive little shrub, and carries pretty, rose-coloured flowers; it grows in desolate regions, and in exposed spots by the shores of the sea, where nothing else will live. The only shelter around, it shielded the ark wherein lay the body of Osiris when it drifted ashore at Byblos. What more natural than that Isis should pick some of its elegant sprays and that the tamarisk should form an emblem of the sepulchral rites that followed. The myrtle performed a similar duty at Eleusis. When the Dionysiac fraternity of builders rehearsed their mysteries at Tyre it is fairly possible to suppose that the tamarisk, the myrtle, or the acacia made an appearance among the ceremonies. It is by no means improbable that when Phales, the relative of King Hiram, was murdered at Tyre, in 917 B.C., that the acacia, the emblem of innocence, was prominently displayed at his obsequies—indeed, it is well within the probabilities of the local circumstances to suppose that it would. The Fraternity had been loyal to King Hiram and were in all likelihood opposed to the treacherous priest who slew the son; in that case the acacia wood, the shittim wood of the Jews, the emblem of innocence, would be worn by the members of the Craft as indicative that they had no share in the death of that just man. It was the acacia, the emblem of innocence, that marked the resting-place of the murdered body of Hiram Abif. The little thread is thickening. If the foregoing suggestion be accepted it leads us straight into a Masonic Lodge in Ancient Tyre, and we have a fair right to conjecture that with the strong bond of tradition it connects Tyre with Etruria, Etruria with Rome, and Rome with France, Germany and England.

Another thread remains; a strong one—the three murderers. The first threatened, the second wounded, and the third killed our Grand Master. What were the three murderers but October, November, and December? and what the death of Hiram Abif but the falling of the sun into the winter solstice?

Surely, the Legend of Hiram Abif has as reliable a foundation as that of any of the other legends that float unquestioned upon the world. The tamarisk shrub, the sprig of acacia, the myrtle of Persephone, the mistletoe of the Scandinavian legend, are all part of one and the same story—Typhon, Pluto, the three murderers, Loki, and Höd personifying the spirit of darkness and evil, whilst Osiris, Persephone, Hiram Abif, and Baldur supply the principle of beneficence and light.

SOLOMON'S TEMPLE EXAGGERATED.

The conclusions to be drawn from what has just passed certainly favour the belief that the constructors of Modern Masonry found the Hiramic Legend awaiting them in a more or less perfect state, possibly colouring it anew in some degree or giving new shape to it in welding together the pieces in which it reached them. But if Anderson and his friends were neither able enough nor, as we may well believe, mischievous enough to forestall Macpherson with a Masonic Ossian, they were certainly guilty of grossly and, viewing the fact that they were Bible scholars, wilfully exaggerating the glories of King Solomon's Temple. The following description, taken from page 12 of the book of the Constitution (1723), exhibits Anderson spurring his loose-reigned Pegasus athwart history with a vengeance, that leaves even that prince among grandiloquent and unreliable boasters, the great Josephus himself, far in the rear:—

"Nor do we read of anything in Caanan so large. The wall that enclosed it being 7,700 feet in compass, far less any holy place fit to be named with it, for exactly proportioned and beautiful dimensions, from the magnificent Porch on the East to the glorious and reverend Sanctum Sanctorum in the West, with most lovely and convenient Apartments for the Kings, Princes, Priests, and Levites, Israelites, and Gentiles also, it being a house of prayer for all nations, and capable of receiving in the Temple proper and in all the courts and apartments together no less than 300,000 people, by a modest calculation allowing a square cubit to each person. And if we consider the 1,453 columns of Parian Marble, with twice as many Pillasters, both having glorious capitals of several orders, and about 2,246 windows, besides those in the Pavement, with the unspeakable and costly decorations of it within (and much more might be found) we must conclude its prospect to transcend our imagination, and that it was justly esteemed by far the finest piece of Masonry on the earth before or since, and the chief wonder of the world, and was dedicated or consecrated in the most solemn manner by King Solomon."

THE BATTLE OF THE ARCHES.

We have dwelt with satisfaction on the grateful point that no attempt was made to force out the great religious convictions of the old Craft when consolidated into the new as the stalking-horse of petty divergencies of creed or as the hobby-holder of either the " real presence " or the doctrine of the " elect." But while speculative Masonry thus kept its ancient way in the purity of simplicity and truth, operative Masonry flung off its coat and leapt down into the arena, a fierce partisan of the " battle of the arches," determined to have a last kick at the despised Gothic, which, still undaunted, reared its noble head at Westminster in the very midst of their heated controversy and contempt.

England, whose architects from the 12th to the end of the 15th century had produced works equalling any to be found elsewhere in the world, began to forget her old models and failed to break out into new forms and fresh contrivances. To anticipate the coming changes we must turn our attention to Italy and the period of Renaissance. In Italy, Gothic art never found a congenial home; being the fashion of the time in other countries, certain, though languid attempts, were made to naturalise it. In 1291, Santa Croce in Florence was designed on Gothic lines, and in 1565 we find Vasari tinkering at Gothic arches in the historic church of Santa Maria Novella, which, with an incredible degradation in art, present the puerile device of sham perspective by narrowing and lowering the arches as they proceed from the west door to the transept—a trick which, with equally unhappy effect, has been resorted to in the side aisles beyond the transept of the magnificent cathedral now in course of erection at Marseilles. But the features of Italian architecture which most caught the taste of the English and took deepest root with their builders were those presented in the works of Andrea Palladio, of Vincenza, 1518-80, the latest artist of the Renaissance period. Anderson in his master's song thus speaks of Palladio:—

> Thus tho' in Italy the Art
>   From Gothic Rubbish first was rais'd;
> And Great Palladio did impart
>   A Style by Mason's justly prais'd:
> Yet here his mighty Rival Jones,
>   Of British Architects the Prime,
> Did build such glorious Heaps of Stones,
>   As ne'er were matched since Cæsar's time.

Palladio, though by no means deserving the name of the regenerator of Italian art, was undoubtedly an artist of very high excellence, his chief characteristics being simplicity and a sparing indulgence of the lavish enrichments in which the early Renaissance was apt to revel. His principal works are in Venice and in his native town, Vincenza; in the latter, in the Palazzo del Consiglio, is a double series of grand and beautiful arcades, built about the middle of the 16th century, and which in great probability served Inigo Jones as a model. Anderson points with much pride to Whitehall and the Banqueting House built by command of James I., and to St Paul's Church, in Covent Garden, " with its glorious portico built by Inigo Jones."

Sir Christopher Wren, whose magnificent Cathedral of St. Paul's is not only, so far as the exterior is concerned, equal but superior to the great Italian churches, comes in for no word of praise or acknowledgment. Though considerably smaller, St. Paul's certainly exhibits a far more beautiful exterior than its Italian prototype, St. Peter's; the severe beauty of its classic lines making it always a matter of deep regret that Sir Christopher Wren had no opportunity to study the remains of the great Greeks, to whose exquisite simplicity and loveliness the spirit of his genius showed so natural a bent.

ANDERSON AS A POET.

That Anderson's knowledge of architecture was well on a par with his performances as a poet the following verses from his " Master's Song " contain the most competent testimony :—

> Oh! glorious days for Masons wise,
>   O'er all the Roman Empire when
> Their Fame resounding to the Skies,
>   Proclaim'd them good and useful Men;
> For many Ages thus employ'd,
>   Until the Goths, with warlike Rage,
> And brutal Ignorance destroy'd
>   The toil of many a learned Age.

But when the conqu'ring Goths were brought
    T' embrace the Christian Faith they found
The folly that their Fathers wrought,
    In loss of Architecture sound.
At length their Zeal for stately Fanes,
    And wealthy Grandeur, when at Peace,
Made them exert their utmost Pains,
    Their Gothic Buildings to upraise.

Thus many a sumptuous lofty Pile
    Was rais'd in every Christian Land,
Tho' not conform to Roman Style,
    Yet which did Reverence command :
The King and Craft agreeing still,
    In well form'd Lodges to supply
The mournful Want of Roman Skill
    With their new sort of Masonry.

For many Ages this prevails,
    Their Work is Architecture deem'd :
In England, Scotland, Ireland, Wales,
    The Craftsmen highly are esteem'd.
By Kings as Masters of the Lodge,
    By many a wealthy noble Peer,
By Lord and Laird, by Priest and Judge,
    By all the People everywhere.

CONCLUSION.

With these views, it is not surprising that in the early forms of the new Masonry we find frequent allusions to "true collonading," and that the device of the "keystone," so important and essential an element in Roman architecture, which may be roughly typified as that of the "round arch," should be elevated into the most dignified attribute of Masonry, passing by and ignoring the science of the progression and proportion of numbers, which is the true base and study of architecture. These things, although of much interest to the Craft in reviewing the historical traditions of Masonry, are, however, of but little practical value. Freemasonry has avowedly departed from its practical or operative platform, no longer do Craftsmen assemble in the Lodge to design and construct edifices which shall be handed down to future generations as exhibitions of genius in conception and of excellence in construction. The needs of the world are changed, and competition has thrown all things open to all men.

Modern Freemasonry is strictly speculative and benevolent. It retains the sublime symbolism we have noted in the east and seen pictured in the mosaic of the ancient Lodge of Pompeii, it holds firm and fast to the simple though complete doctrine of the Great Architect of the Universe, it inculcates maxims of virtue and benevolence, and it may be said with the most perfect truth that he who is a good Mason is a good man.

We have thus arrived at a position in which we may fairly take leave of our subject. We have followed the symbols of Masonry from the farthest times of antiquity, through the intervening ages, down to their identical use in the Freemasonry of to-day. We have followed the course of the great Allegory, Myth or Legend from its primal origin, through several of its collateral branches, and have connected it with the great central legend of Freemasonry. Each circumstance of value has been more or less touched upon, pointing out the lines on which further study and investigation may be advantageously prosecuted, exhibiting the high value of Freemasonry to the world as the teacher of pure and simple doctrine, and, as an unbroken chain, holding us in direct contact with the wisdom and learning of antiquity.

In conclusion, we may justly use the words of Tertullian's picture of the early churches of Christianity, and say, the Masonic Fraternity is a society united together in "the communion of peace, the title of brotherhood, the token of hospitality, and the tradition of one faith."

APPENDIX.

Note to page 30.—The following account of the Persian traditions concerning the Sun in Leo greatly strengthens the argument of R. H. Brown, the authority for the statement in the text. It appears in Fellow's History of Freemasonry, p. 231, and is by that author attributed to Sir John Malcolm, chap. xxv. :—

"The Shahs of Persia have for many years preserved, as the peculiar arms of their country, the sign or figure of Sol in the constellation of Leo, and this device, exhibiting a Lion couchant and the sun rising at his back, has not only been quartered upon their escutcheons and embroidered on their banners, but has been converted into an Order, which in the form of gold and silver medals has been given to those who have distinguished themselves against the enemies of their country."

Note to page 59.—In Fergusson's "Holy Sepulchre" we read the following comment on the size of Solomon's Temple :—"Most of our London Churches, such for instance as St. Martin's-in-the-Fields, are both as to dimensions and lithic ornament larger and more splendid than King Solomon's Temple."

Note to page 73.—Max Mueller in his lecture on the Vedas, says :—"Though not expressly asserted anywhere, a belief in personal immortality is taken for granted in several passages of the Old Testament, and we can hardly think of Abraham or Moses as without a belief in life and immortality."

We read further on this subject in the "Life of St. Paul," by Rev. J. Conybeare and the Very Rev. J. S. Howson:—"The belief in a future state may be said to have been an open question among the Jews, when our Lord appeared and 'brought life and immortality to light,' we find the Sadducees established in the highest offices of the priesthood, and possessed of the greatest power in the Sanhedrim, and yet they did not believe in any future state, nor in any spiritual existence independent of the body.

Note to page 100.—"The façade of Notre Dame of Poitiers has two columns, it having conical summits and resembling Boaz and Jachin. Founded 1161." Fergusson's "Handbook of Architecture."

Note to page 134.—A curious article appeared in the columns of the "Gentleman's Magazine" for 1753, purporting to give the text of a document discovered by John Locke in 1696, wherein a series of questions and answers concerning the practice of Masonry in the time of Henry VI. were set forth. The article in question was accepted by the Freemasons and appeared with due sanction in "Anderson's Constitutions, revised, enlarged and brought down to the year 1784, under the direction of the Hall Committee, by John Noorthouck." Modern historians are, however, unanimous in condemning it as spurious, and its introduction into the text would consequently serve no good purpose. The document is spoken of as the Locke-Leyland MS.

Crests, Arms, Monograms, &c., Plain or Illuminated,
for Lodge Notepaper, &c.

Printed in the United States
85875LV00004B/322-324/A